Praise

When 10+ years have passed since your last academic public speaking class, this resource goes above and beyond to boost your confidence while setting you up to tell the story you want. After taking on a new position that puts me at the forefront of delivering speeches and speaking to wide audiences, I am grateful to have gained insight into growing as a speaker. Now, a year and a half later, I feel I have regained my confidence in sharing my words.
Emily M. Winters
President, Northwest Chamber of Commerce

Public speaking to me is about giving. It is about sharing knowledge that you have to make someone else's life better or easier. I highly encourage you to get out your highlighter and take notes on these tips to help your fear [of public speaking], which affects about 75% of the population. Reflect on the fact that it is your duty to share your gift with others, to educate, and make the world a better place. Thank you, David, for sharing this book and your wisdom.
Kimberly Chmiel
Learning and Development Specialist

I have had the amazing opportunity to elevate my speaking skills and confidence through training from David and the DSB Leadership Group. I have taken what I have learned to excel in speaking opportunities across several platforms. No matter how old or young you are, you will find real value in this book that can be applied to your life so you can reach your career goals.
Corey'L Sams
Entrepreneur, Founder of CRE82INSPIRE

Troy

Keep Spin

TALK IT UP!
A Guide To Successful Public Speaking

DAVID SUK BROWN & DANNY SUK BROWN

Talk It Up! A Guide To Successful Public Speaking
Copyright © 2022 by Danny Suk Brown & David Suk Brown

All rights reserved, including the right to reproduce this book or portion thereof in any form whatsoever. For information, address:

David Suk Brown
http://www.dsbleadershipgroup.com/
Instagram: @dsbleadershipgroup
Instagram: @twinstalkitup
Twitter: @dsbleadership
Facebook: facebook.com/dsbleadership/
Facebook: facebook.com/twinstalkitup

Every attempt has been made to source all quotes correctly.

Scriptures are taken from the Holy Bible, New International Version®, NIV®. Copyright © 1973, 1978, 1984, 2011 by Biblica, Inc.™ Used by permission of Zondervan. All rights reserved worldwide. www.zondervan.com The "NIV" and "New International Version" are trademarks registered in the United States Patent and Trademark Office by Biblica, Inc.™

Canva designs are used within their legal commercial license, stated within their agreement, seen here:
"Content licenses and using Canva for commercial purposes." *Canva*, https://www.canva.com/help/article/licenses-copyright-legal-commercial-use/. Accessed 21 April 2022.

For additional copies or bulk purchases visit:
David Suk Brown's Amazon Author Page
https://www.amazon.com/author/davidsukbrown

ISBN: 9798811623990

Printed in the United States of America.

This book is dedicated to our wives Leslie Brown and Jenny Brown. You have blessed us with your love and a continued belief that we are created to make an impact. You inspire and strengthen us to speak.

Contents

FOREWORD	[i]
INTRODUCTION	[iii]
CHAPTER 1: Why Public Speaking	[1]
CHAPTER 2: Forms Of Communication	[9]
CHAPTER 3: Aspects Of Public Speaking	[21]
CHAPTER 4: The Power Of Visualization	[33]
CHAPTER 5: Dealing With Speaking Anxiety A.K.A. Nerves	[39]
CHAPTER 6: Say It In A Sentence: Create & Structure	[47]
CHAPTER 7: Rehearse, Then Crush	[57]
CHAPTER 8: Master Fillers & Vocal Variety	[63]
CHAPTER 9: Storytelling	[69]
CHAPTER 10: To Tech Or Not To Tech	[73]
CHAPTER 11: Impromptu Talks	[81]
CHAPTER 12: Handling Questions & Awards	[89]
CONCLUSION	[99]
WORKSHOP 1 | Imposter Syndrome	[101]
WORKSHOP 2 | What Pros Do And Don't Do	[107]
WORKSHOP 3 | Elevator Pitch	[111]
WORKSHOP 4 | Speaking With The C-Suite	[115]
WORKSHOP 5 | Virtual Ice Breakers	[119]
WORKSHOP 6 | Your Speaker SWOT Analysis	[121]
WORKSHOP 7 | Your Affirmation List	[125]
ACKNOWLEDGEMENTS	[127]
ABOUT THE AUTHORS	[129]
WAYS TO FIND DANNY & DAVID	[131]
ENDNOTES	[133]
ADDITIONAL RESOURCES	[139]
INDEX	[141]

Foreword

There's an ancient story about two men who went to a place called Iconium (*Acts* 14:1) (Iconium is the Latin name of the ancient city of Konya, in Turkey) and there they spoke so powerfully and with such conviction that people believed in what they were saying! It's incredible to think that as humans our minds can be changed (even if we believe something different) through the power of speech.

Consider these ancient sayings:
- "The tongue has the power of life and death." *Proverbs* 18:21
- "Grasp the subject, the words will follow." - Cato, The Elder[1]
- "Rhetoric is the art of ruling the minds of men." - Plato[2]

Now consider what these sayings mean. Words coming from our mouths are powerful! They can inspire the heart or cut it deeply. Think about the times when you've been inspired by a teacher or a well-placed speech in a movie or maybe someone who said something critical and how deeply it hurt you. There's power in speech, either positive or negative. Or what Cato the Elder says in the second quote; "Grasp the subject, the words will follow."

I have been speaking publicly for over thirty years and it's true that when you really grasp a particular subject, I mean really own it, then the words will follow. As I teach public speaking, I always have students speak first about themselves for five minutes. Why? Because that's a subject they really know! How many are in your family? Where are you from? What do you like to do? What places have you visited? What did you like about them? What's your favorite movie? Even though people are nervous even when speaking about themselves they usually are not as nervous and the information flows freely. The more you own a topic the less nervous you're going to be and this book will give insight into this.

In the third quote you may be thinking well I'm not into ruling the minds of men but when you're speaking publicly you are trying to influence people. You may be called on to just give information, persuade your team or inspire minds and the better you understand the approaches of public speaking the better you'll be at reaching your goal.

"There are always three speeches, for every one you actually gave.
The one you practiced, the one you gave, and the one you wish you gave."[3]
DALE CARNEGIE

Understanding the nuances of speaking is going to help you to be better at giving the speech you want to give. As you practice, you'll get better, have more confidence, and be more adept at speaking and the insight and ideas that Danny and Dave share in the book will help you get the job done. I've known these men for over twenty-seven years, and they've come a long way themselves in speaking. Through trial and error, knowledge, understanding, and getting the feedback they've grown in their confidence in public speaking and what they'll be sharing is not THEORY but what actually works!

Their stories and real-life experiences are a result of their perseverance, so as they give you guidance, it's coming from an authentic place. Whether it's a business presentation for your company, speaking at a conference, or making a memorable wedding toast you'll find the information and tips a great help. Enjoy!

They are men of integrity, and excellence and have a great work ethic. The information that you're getting will definitely be a great guide for increasing your public speaking ability.

Steven Cannon, author of *Guru Wisdom*[4]

Introduction

Do you want to improve or master your communication and public speaking skills? Do you want to overcome your fear of speaking? Want to nail down that next big presentation? This one skill set can be the most important factor in the growth of your professional career? If you have ever asked yourself any of these questions, then this is the perfect guide for you.

Why did we write a book on public speaking? We wanted to listen to our clients as well as family and friends who asked us to put some of our public speaking training into a book. It was almost overwhelming the amount of support and encouragement we received for this project. We also felt it was important to share a little about our journey to becoming speaking coaches. We were those students who in high school and college would use this skill to run for office. We were those young leaders who would rely on this skill set to advance our careers and be advocates in our communities.

Great leadership requires effective communication and being able to speak with confidence is a vital component of that. Improving your public speaking will increase your ability to sell more, inspire more and boost your career.

Business deals can be won or lost based on how the presenter is perceived. Personal satisfaction and business success can depend so much on the presenter's ability to clearly communicate. Even the great Warren Buffet stated that this was the most important skill for a professional and that this one skill could increase their overall value by 50%.[1]

Many assume when you say public speaking, that you are either a professional full-time motivational speaker or a clergy member (such as a minister, priest, rabbi, or khalif). Public speaking is so much more than that and it is not reserved for a select few. Whether you are speaking to an audience of one or a crowd of 5,000, you are speaking, and this material can support you.

According to research, glossophobia, also known as the fear of public speaking, is the greatest fear. It is a phobia that is believed to affect up to 75% of the population.[2] There is an adage that some would rather be in the coffin than delivering the eulogy. There are so many opportunities waiting should you choose to take the stage. We do not want fear, or a lack of confidence to hold you back. You have a message and others need to hear it.

Here is a fact that needs to be stated: we are not born effective and powerful speakers. Here is another fact: we can grow in this skill as it can be learned. Great public speakers like Les Brown, Tony Robbins, Eric Thomas, and even former President Barack Obama have worked hard to master their techniques. They constantly train and practice their craft to the point where it can seem like second nature. They may invest in books, courses, seminars, and even work with coaches like us.

We started our company *DSB Leadership Group*[3] to help professionals grow in their confidence, and overcome speaking anxieties by developing the right mindset, grasping, and practicing public speaking techniques. We do this because we believe that every professional can increase their ability to influence through growing this ever-important skill. There is a great joy we have when we learn that those we support become more effective communicators.

Keep in mind that public speaking has so many advantages. Your journey starts with a decision that you are going to invest in yourself - to invest in your public speaking growth. Your *Guide to Successful Public Speaking* is designed to help both the newbie as well as the seasoned professional learn and develop the right mindset regardless of their background in speaking.

Welcome to *Talk It Up, A Guide To Successful Public Speaking*!

CHAPTER 1
Why Public Speaking

"Speech is power: speech is to *persuade*, to *convert*, to *compel*."[1]
RALPH WALDO EMERSON

What is public speaking and what occasions might present themselves that require you to speak? Whatever your answer, public speaking is really a matter of influence. This is true whether you are trying to convey an idea or just having a simple conversation.

The purpose of public speaking typically falls into four areas:
1. *Inform*
2. *Persuade* or convince
3. *Entertain* or inspire
4. *Meet* a need, specifically, a need that only you can fill

If you are in a position where you interact with team members, leadership, or clients, then you have a golden opportunity to improve your public speaking. This art and skill helped us become more compelling and effective communicators. It helped to strengthen our leadership

Far too many people never realize the importance of developing their communication skills until they are asked to. For example:
- *Deliver* a wedding toast.
- *Lead* a team discussion.
- *Represent* your organization at a trade show.
- *Speak* at a conference.
- *Introduce* a speaker or presenter.
- *Present* a sales pitch.
- *Participate* and sit on a discussion panel.
- *Share* a "few words."

Aside from any of the scenarios listed above, you may have your own reasons for wanting to speak up. Perhaps you want to:
- *Advance* a personal cause or champion an idea.
- *Motivate* and inspire others.
- *Gain* greater visibility within your organization or community.
- *Overcome* your own insecurities with "taking the stage."

Modes Of Persuasion: Ethos, Pathos & Logos
The Greek philosopher Aristotle, who was taught by Plato, developed what we would call, the modes of persuasion. According to the Stanford Encyclopedia of Philosophy, "The systematical core of Aristotle's *Rhetoric* is the doctrine that there are three technical means of persuasion."[2] (For more information, see our 'Additional Resources' section in the back of this book.)

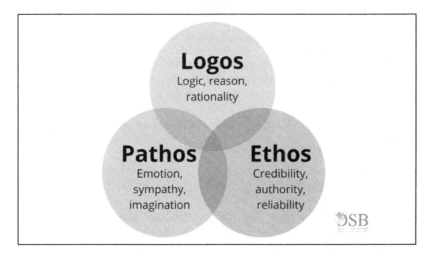

Before we dive into this, let's paint a few scenarios that may have been a reality for many of you. When was the last time you had to get an important deal signed? What about a key project that you had to get across the finish line? When was the last time you were in a position where you had to persuade or win people over to your side? How frustrating was it when this could not get done? Did you ever walk away thinking that you missed it; that you missed the opportunity?

Consider our children who really want something. They know the decision-maker well enough to implement one of or a combination of Ethos, Pathos, or Logos. When all else fails, they look up, with those big 'puppy dog' eyes and adorable faces. How can we not give in? They are so adorable and the masters of Ethos, Pathos, and Logos.

It's time to tap into that and learn how to use and integrate the three modes of persuasion into your conversations. Mastering these will enable you to become more successful as a leader and as a speaker. Public speaking and presentation skills are all about influence. If you can appeal to your audience, you can win more opportunities and deals. One or two of these might seem more natural and comfortable for you, but you should strongly consider the importance of learning the art of using all three.

Ethos

How can you increase your effectiveness to convince? A speaker would use ethos to show the audience that they are a credible source and worth listening to. Ethos is the Greek word for "character." The word "ethic" is derived from ethos. Ethos reflects your credibility. As a leader, speaker, and presenter, you should ask yourself, "How credible am I?" What's your reputation within your community, workplace, or school? Why would anyone want to listen to you? For example, I (David) bring over 26 years of speaking experience as a speaker and speaking coach. Wouldn't you feel more confident working with someone with that background compared to someone who started only a year ago? Your credibility is crucial.

We don't want you to feel tempted to throw out your resume or toot your own horn before you begin speaking or delivering your presentation. A better approach is to tactfully have yourself introduced so that you are not 'tooting your own horn' and it would make sense. Let's face it, you are most likely already on the program and people can read on their own. You can employ, if needed, another professional, host, emcee, or even the event organizer to introduce you. They can share a little bit about you. Be confident as you are speaking for a reason. You're worth listening to and your credibility has already been established.

Use Ethos as an appeal to win arguments or to increase your influence; all this is based on credibility.

Pathos

Another aspect of persuasion we want to introduce is pathos. Pathos is the ability to appeal based on emotion. As we already alluded to, this is what many children are good at. They can make you feel guilty, or they can make you feel like you're the greatest. Who would not want to be known as the greatest ever? Speakers can use pathos to invoke sympathy from an audience. Pathos is the Greek root word for both "suffering" and "experience."

Even after 23 years of marriage, I (David) think about that endless 'Honey to Do List'. The list never seems to go away. It's the little things she does and says that work on my ego as well as my genuine desire to make her smile. She's using this mode of persuasion. She's appealing based on emotion. Although I've never built anything in my life, I feel stirred up so therefore I want to do it. I feel like I should, at the very minimum, attempt to tackle these projects.

Consider some of the greatest leaders or advocates throughout human history. Without a doubt, they knew how to use this mode of persuasion. It's an art. If applied correctly, you will influence people and therefore lead them toward thought as well as action. From what you may have heard in sales or related training workshops, people often buy on emotion. Yes, sometimes there's buyer's remorse, But, in most cases, when a purchase is made, based on emotion, the general feeling is that you 'had to have it'. You needed it and somehow it completed you.

Why does it seem that late-night TV is the best or most opportune time marketers use to place those commercials of animals in need or children in need? You are likely to hear something along the lines of, 'for just a cup of coffee a day, you can make the difference'. An appeal is being made based on emotion. This could be one of the most effective tools for closing more deals.

Consider metaphors. Consider stories. If you could master the use of metaphors and storytelling, it will position you for incredible success. People want to know you and stories are a great method for connecting with your listeners and for giving them a part of you.

Being deliberate about marketing, even in its simplest form, can be suggestive. And, furthermore, it even plays on our emotional triggers or perceived needs. For children, it may be the same tactic ice cream trucks use when playing that iconic melody. Why? As soon as you hear the melody, you start looking for your wallet or you run to a parent with your hands out in expectation. The melody stirs up the emotions of what it's going to feel like to get that nice cold treat.

Logos
The third mode of persuasion is Logos. Logos is the Greek word for 'word', and yet it means so much more. There is much more depth to this word, and it goes beyond just saying this means "logical". Speakers use logos as a means to convince an audience in a fine-tuned argument or reason by the use of logic or reason. Using theoretical or abstract language, including citing facts, using data, history and literal analogies are essential for this. This is where I (Danny) would say equates to logical, factual arguments.

Never undervalue the importance of doing and using research! I (Danny) often utilize facts and statistics to strengthen my position. It can be very difficult to argue against numbers. Consider when you are giving a speech or some type of presentation, and you share something along the lines of, 'four out of five doctors recommend this', or 'based on a poll (Gallup poll), 85% of the people said they preferred online banking with a Mobile App'. When you start using research like this, it has the potential to persuade people. They are led to believe or think that what is being presented is a point worth considering. They may even think that 'if so, many people believe that', then, they should of course do the same. Perhaps they will be swayed to go down that same path of thinking. You're using logic, which is the reason you ought to do your research. Doesn't this make sense? Doesn't this imply x? Or doesn't this imply why? When you do that, it all makes perfect sense.

Let's consider another illustration. Imagine while investigating a crime scene, you discover fingerprints, strands of hair, and some form of bodily fluids. When you are brought in as an expert, you may present before the jury the results of your findings and reveal from the evidence, in the form of fingerprints and DNA, who could be the likely culprit. Boom, that's a fine-sounding argument!

Concluding The Modes Of Persuasion
The above-mentioned are concepts that you should strongly consider implementing into your strategy. It most certainly will aid you. We addressed what Ethos is and how you could use this in your presentation. If you are just starting out, you could do this solely based on your history, simply because this is a reflection (or rather an indication) of your reputation. You could do it based on your title. You could do this based on whatever you believe establishes your credibility. Why would they want to trust you? Why should they even listen to you? This is essential. For example, 'In all my years as a Marine' or 'It took me 27 years to attain this level'. Your audience may be moved by the fact that you have experience or knowledge. You're worth listening to as you are the subject matter expert.

When you think about what could pull at your heartstrings aka emotions, this is Pathos. We love to hear the stories about unsung heroes or about the underdog who overcomes unbelievable odds to win it all. You could share about your involvement and work within your community, with the food or toy drives, with the PTA, or with other volunteer work. Sharing personally can help people feel connected to you.

Logos is about appealing by reason, right? Those who love numbers and 'facts' appreciate this approach. The data always seems to make something so clear that you cannot possibly argue against it. You are making the appeal based on logic and reasoning, thus showing this position, based on history, decisively furthers your ability to persuade.

I (David) was watching a documentary on the Netherlands and how they try to fight back the rise in water levels and the potential for flooding. I was amazed by the documentary and how they dedicate so many resources to address this concern and, dare I say, the reality. They have implemented systems and specialized structures with ingenious engineering and, as a result, they have not really suffered a major flood in over 60 years.

[5]

Perhaps these are some strategies that could be implemented in areas around the world with heavily populated centers near flood zones. The argument could be along the lines of, 'sea waters are rising, which will lead to an increase of x amount more flooding, which means y number of lives threatened and z amount of economic losses. Based on that, it makes sense to implement and invest in *blank* million to build this structure.

It's about persuading. It's about moving people. It's about saying, "I've seen this in business." How did that make you feel? Are you dissatisfied? Are you frustrated yet? You need to do this right now! You're making people respond based on feeling. As a side note, I (David) want you to work on these things. Feel free to reach out to me and I will gladly help you to construct your presentation.

Benefits

There are so many benefits from cultivating your ability to deliver authentic and powerful speeches and presentations. One of these key benefits is around conquering speaking anxiety and growing in your confidence. Another benefit is that you are now adding another tool to your leadership toolbox. Leaders are always looking for ways to grow and develop their leadership skills.

Consider how the causes or organizations you are passionate about can be advanced through your ability to influence your audience. Think about how your audience will leave transformed as a direct result of your presentation or speech. Think about how growth in this area will impact your professional career and bring about greater visibility and opportunities.

We strongly encourage you to internalize this conviction: PUBLIC SPEAKING IS ALL ABOUT INFLUENCE. We want to help you find your voice and increase your influence. Whether you need a complete mind shift or just some polishing, this guide will support you in your growth journey. There are some who may not understand the value of this skill and yet there are sales professionals who attend and invest thousands in sales training. Why do they do this? They do this because they believe in learning effective techniques and being around others who are just as driven. Furthermore, they are convinced that it will aid their effectiveness in sales, as well as in advancing their career goals. Should you not also have the same attitude with your public speaking skills?

We want you to look at every opportunity you must present and share on 'your stage'. We want your audience to hear not only the message, but we also want them to hear you - your heart and what you stand for. You have something to say, and they need to hear it! Be a compelling communicator and tell them something - something that only you can say.

Talk It Up! - A Guide To Successful Public Speaking

Consider that somebody must do it and that somebody can be you. That somebody should be you. Think about what's at stake. Consider what would be gained by using your voice. While there are others who can deliver a similar speech or message, there is only one you. Your experiences, your talents, and your heart are needed. Your audience is waiting for you. Your audience needs you. Don't concern yourself with anything other than the impact you will have and the way your audience will be shaped by you. Graciously and generously give.

"All great speakers were bad speakers at first."[3]
RALPH WALDO EMERSON

It may take time, but you will eventually get there. You only get better when you continue to speak and speak often. Think about any activity, whether that be music, sports, or a valued skill; you become a better speaker by working on it - by speaking more often. So, do not neglect practice as practice presents an opportunity to improve and gain both confidence and exposure. Believe in yourself and in what you are presenting. Remember, that you have something to say, and your audience needs to hear that message from you.

Example: John, a well-respected business owner avoided publicly addressing his company and would often have his COO or Director of Communications deliver updates, news, and announcements. He never lacked conviction with the direction of his company but was paralyzed by the thought of standing before the sea of gazing eyes. He would imagine his employees not seeing him as a strong leader and losing respect for him.

Consider for a moment that you are John. Sure, you could try and justify not wanting to speak before your organization as a 'way to let others shine' or assume that they know you are a strong leader. Why would it matter to you or your employees if you spoke? It could mean everything - from employee retention to an increase in overall productivity. Never forget why your voice is so important to those who need to hear from you.

John eventually realized that at the end of the day, his employees needed to hear his voice—they needed to hear him speak.

He began to accept that the pain of losing them (to competitors or to a decrease in productivity) was greater than the pain of delivering a message. He made a commitment to be courageous and get open about his fears. He practiced and eventually began to speak more often. His employees appreciated this and even though John is not on the speaking circuit, you can bet that when he speaks, others listen.

[7]

Talk It Up! - A Guide To Successful Public Speaking

Activity
1. *Write* out why you want to speak and why you want to grow in your speaking skills.
2. *List* potential opportunities where you may be able to speak.
3. *Learn* from your favorite speakers while staying true to your voice.
4. *Watch* professionally produced discussions and talks online, and/or listen to programs such as Twins Talk it Up.

CHAPTER 2
Forms Of Communication

"If you can't communicate, it's like winking at a girl in the dark."[1]
WARREN BUFFETT

Communication skills are essential for healthy, efficient, and successful relationships, and workplaces, and for maximizing your career growth opportunities. Some would categorize public speaking or communication at this level as soft skills or interpersonal skills.

An experienced speaker will understand how to best utilize the three forms of communication (verbal, nonverbal, and visual) to maximize their platform. Some might include the written word (as well as braille and symbols) as a fourth area of communication. In the hands of brilliant marketing minds, written communication can be a very effective tool (i.e., blogs, websites, and social media platforms). For the sake of this book, we will concentrate on the first three.

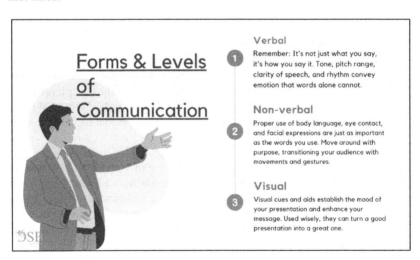

An effective speaker considers both their audience and the objective of the message. When putting together their speech or presentation, they need to evaluate how to create the right balance between these three forms of communication.

Verbal Communication
This first form of communication represents the words that are being used to deliver meaning, transfer information, or convey a message. Success in this area involves the ability to properly manage and use the spoken language including grammar, the pace of speech, and tonality. Words do indeed have 'power' and must be handled both accurately and correctly.

While verbal is what you say, vocal is how you say it. Speech is a powerful tool for building connectivity and trust. The pitch and tone of someone's voice, the speed and rhythm of the spoken word, and the pauses between those words can express more than what is being communicated by words alone.

How you say your message is just as important as the message itself. Notice the following statement, "there is a fire" vs "THERE IS A FIRE!". The way in which these identical statements would be received changes with the emphasis. How you say your message drastically impacts and affects your audience.

Verbal communication also encompasses your tone, pitch range, clarity of your speech, and even the rhythm and speed of your speech. In terms of vocal variety - can you fluctuate your range? In our training sessions, we talk about the difference between projecting and yelling. Projecting is controlled while yelling is using your "outside voice."

Turn Up Or Down The Volume
Vocal inflection is important because speaking in a monotone is like inviting your audience to fall asleep. Instead, you need to strategically alter your range with each segment of communication. Have you ever seen the Clear Eyes Drops Commercials with Ben Stein[2]? His catchword is very simple, "Wow." While it works quite well in the context of the advertisement, imagine listening to a 30-minute presentation with this delivery.

Your tone of voice can be correlated to the 'music of your voice'. Fluctuating your tone can draw an audience in and it can even provide a charge for them to go out. Can you learn to use both your inside voice and outside voice? You not only need to consider the tone of your voice, but you may also need to consider the pace or speed at which you speak. This will reflect or highlight the emphasis on what is being said.

Without vocal variety[3], your audience may be led to a state of being bored and lose attention or focus as the message will be perceived as being flat. Imagine a movie or a performance without a variety of volume, tone, and inflection and you will find yourself sleeping until you get that elbow in your rib section from your significant other to 'pay attention'. We suggest that you stay away from a big meal if this is the type of evening entertainment you are expecting.

Talk It Up! - A Guide To Successful Public Speaking

In the same way, your volume, tone, and inflection must change throughout your presentation. How else can you convey excitement if you do not reflect this with your voice? There are times when changing the speed or pace of your delivery can add to the impact and desired effect of your story or the point you are wanting the audience to walk away with.

All these techniques will make your message more interesting as they will captivate your audience. Try reading a sentence, paragraph, or story with these techniques in mind. First, speak softly and see if this would 'draw' people in, and then read it loudly. Next, try speaking at a fast rate or pace and then read that same sentence, paragraph, or story very slowly. Notice the difference.

You are going to see an emphasis throughout this book on how important it is to keep your audience in the front of your mind. Your audience will also dictate how to best utilize verbal communication. This includes the use of jargon, grammar, and how you articulate your words. This will also determine whether you can be a little more animated or should I say exaggerated. Please note that all of this can be done without losing who you are, without losing your own speaking style. We teach and preach authenticity.

As was stated earlier, words have power. The book of *Proverbs* says, "the tongue has the power of life and death, and those who love it will eat its fruit." (*Proverbs* 18:20). There is a saying that goes something like this: 'the tongue has no bones but can break a heart. So be careful with your words'. Remember that once they leave your mouth, you cannot take them back. But they can shut down wars or ignite a dream.

Here are some things to keep in mind with verbal communication that may give you an advantage the next time you speak. Be confident and use the entire 'Toolbox'. Speak with clarity and with confidence. Later in this guidebook, we will introduce what we often refer to as the power of the pause. We will also tackle how to avoid the use of filler words.

Nonverbal Communication
The second form of communication does not use words to convey meaning. When we think of nonverbal, we typically think of body language. Success for a speaker in this area would include being in 'touch' with or aware of how you are using your body, including your facial expressions to influence and connect with your audience.

Nonverbal communication is often communicated through facial expressions, hand gestures, posture, and even appearance. It can be both intentional and unintentional and can convey a variety of signals and messages. These nonverbal elements can aid or hurt the presentation as we are instinctually

Talk It Up! - A Guide To Successful Public Speaking

heightened to what is presented and an audience's radar may alert them to receiving something incredible or to the danger of unwanted material or information.

How do we use our body to effectively communicate our message? Is moving about or pacing on stage an effective method? You do not necessarily have to move or pace when you are speaking but if you do, it is possible that your movement can become distracting. Move with a purpose as to the chalkboard or some illustration or even to ensure every part of the room feels you are speaking to them.

It's Written All Over Your Face
When was the last time you considered what type of message your face was giving to everyone else in the room? We may not notice what our face 'looks like' when we are in a rested place/relaxed state nor the expression or message that is given. We hate to bring this up, but there is something commonly known as, well we will leave the acronym and you can choose to look it up. It is RBF or what we can characterize as "resting face syndrome". This is a facial expression that often is unintentional and gives off the appearance or impression that a person is angry, annoyed, irritated, or unconcerned. This concept has been studied by psychologists, scientists, and communication experts. Believe it or not, there is a specialty field of study on the face, its muscles, and what they communicate. Think facial recognition software and facial recognition experts.

We had an incredible guest on our Twins Talk it Up Podcast, episode 24 with Facial Expression expert Dan Hill[4]. Dan is the President of Sensory Logic[5], and he is a certified expert on facial decoding, having the ability to identify and capture emotions. He trains and speaks on how you can quantify 'gut reactions', based on peoples' facial expressions. In essence, he shared that there are 23 expressions on the face that reveal seven core emotions. Muscle movement in the face will reflect interest level and this can help executives close more deals.

With this understanding, experts can tell if someone is telling the truth and being genuine. This has served both world leaders and great business influencers alike. This is where you can learn to go deeper than what's verbally being said. So, take time to look in the mirror or ask those you trust to 'catch you' when you are in a relaxed state or mood. You may be surprised to learn that your face may convey something different than what you are feeling or thinking

Your face also needs to convey confidence, and positive energy, and be perceived as friendly and non-threatening. A simple smile can be a disarming and inviting technique. Don't forget to smile and watch how a room can brighten with energy and engagement. It lets your audience know that you are

[12]

Talk It Up! - A Guide To Successful Public Speaking

happy to be there with them. So, smile more often as it takes less energy ala your facial muscles to smile than to frown.

Look Me In The Eye
Tell us if you've heard these before:

- "I asked him to look me in the eye if he has something to say".
- "I can't believe you can look me in the eye and still lie".
- "I wasn't afraid to look him in the eye and speak my truth".

When you hear this phrase, 'look me in the eye', you are reminded of the importance of making eye contact. Eye contact is important and is vital for connecting with your audience and for conveying confidence. Presenters who understand this, are intentional with making eye contact. They are perceived to be friendly, sociable, and ultimately more trustworthy.

When making eye contact, keep in mind that you are in the observation mode as much as your audience is. They need to see and believe that they are important and that they are your focus. Believe us when we say that an audience can sense if you are there for them, so be intentional and meaningful with your eye contact. Remember not to 'stare' but to engage with your eyes.

Don't be that presenter who never 'looks up' nor looks at the audience. If they have their eyes and attention fixated on their notes, the floor, or at the table, then understand that this will affect his credibility and eventually lead to listeners feeling unimportant or even uncertain. We provide training on how to deliver what is commonly known as elevator pitches. One of the points we make is for our clients to understand that what they communicate can make others feel.

Eye contact anxiety[6] can interfere with being able to make and maintain good eye contact. How can shy, anxious speakers overcome this aspect of communication? This fear can be evident when a presenter avoids making eye contact, consistently looks down, or quickly looks away. There are so many thoughts on how to best address and navigate this. They may feel as though they are being judged, become fearful, and lose their thought process. May we suggest a few ways to support this need for connectivity while you are speaking (and listening):

Look at some of the 'friendly' faces that you've made a connection with (preferably before you present). This could prove invaluable and become a proven strategy for counteracting anxiety.

Pick three points within the room: one on the *left*, one in the *middle*, and one on the *right*.

[13]

Rotate your gaze while you are speaking to those three points as this will give the audience a feeling of you being present.

If you feel as if you need to avoid direct eye contact, consider looking near their eyes. You can look at their foreheads or if they are wearing glasses, at the brim of the frame. This will convey that you are interested in them.

The Stare Down
Let's talk about eye contact a bit more.

In much of the Animal kingdom, we commonly see a stare-down of sorts taking place. We watch National Geographic, Animal Planet, or documentaries on the animal kingdom and when you see two creatures staring at each other, you know that it's about to go down. There is going to be a fight for dominance and often for mating privileges.

Boxing, MMA, and martial arts competitions also utilize this, what can be called a technique and opportunity, to generate more hype before a fight. Think about how before the bout even begins, there is that stare down between combatants. The drama starts at the weigh-in and then we see this intensity when the judge or ref gives direction before the fight.

They look each other in the eyes. It may seem innocent or even playful, but it is anything but that. Why: It's more than just an intimidation factor. It is pure psychological warfare. You want to destroy their ego and confidence before the bout even begins. You must win here first before you go into the ring.

We watch these incredible athletes put their minds and bodies on the line for sport and entertainment. I (David) once heard an MMA fighter share that he could learn a lot about his opponent from the stare down. He wanted to see if he could win, even before he had to win again in the ring. He wanted to see if there was a difference in the stare down during the weigh-in and press interviews compared to the first look when he is in the ring receiving directions from the referee.

What does this have to do with Public Speaking? Have you ever been to a conference or sitting at a sales meeting only to be addressed by someone who never looked up or looked at you? How did that make you feel? A confident look has a way of inspiring confidence in others. Never miss the stare down. Someone is going to win, and it better be you.

Misconceptions & Bad Teaching
There are some common myths and poor teaching around this subject as it pertains to curbing speaking anxiety. You may have heard someone teach or share that a way to become a better speaker would be to 'imagine people naked or in their underwear'. Why would we want to do that? That can be creepy and

Talk It Up! - A Guide To Successful Public Speaking

send the wrong vibes. That is just weird to think that a crowd of people with little to no clothes somehow will be less threatening than a room of professionally dressed leaders.

Please do not follow this poor direction often given to see the crowd as "little babies". How can you take your material and presentation seriously if you are imaging the audience as babies? You surely don't speak with infants and young children in the same manner, tone, and emphasis as you would speaking with adults. Your audience would prefer to be addressed with respect and professionalism.

What can you do to convey connection? What can you do to combat these poor teaching or training tips? Acknowledge what is true. The audience is not a threat, and the audience wants you to succeed. They value their time and believe that they can leave your presence with more value, insight, encouragement, and direction because of being with you. We certainly don't want to be made to feel as if we are being looked upon as if we are naked.

Make a gesture such as nodding your head as this will show agreement or understanding. This will then allow you to slowly move your eye contact to another person or another part of the room. The nodding of your head will also build what we call "buy-in" and agreement. You will be perceived more favorably.

There is incredible power when you choose to not avoid the eyes of your audience. There is a difference between making eye contact, looking into the eyes of your audience, and staring at someone, which can make everyone uncomfortable.

Watch Your Hands
Have you ever heard it being said that someone speaks with their hands? Is it distracting? Does it help or support you as the speaker? What should you do with your arms and with your hands? We will address your arms in a moment, but for now, let's address your hands. You may be someone who tends to 'speak with your hands'. You could also be that person who has never really considered what their hands and arms are doing when they are speaking. Should you clasp them, hide them, or overcompensate for what you may feel you are lacking and flare them all over the place? Well, let's get this out of the way. Overuse of them can hurt and affect the effectiveness of your message.

We also do not want you to be the speaker who removes their hands from their pockets only to place them on their hips. When your hands are on your hips, you may come across as disapproving, impatient, and tend to look overbearing.

Some of you reading this may be more of a Star Wars fanatic, while others aligned more with Star Trek. Should you be a 'Trekkie', note that you are not

[15]

Talk It Up! - A Guide To Successful Public Speaking

Spock[7] and so, it does very little to support your intelligence or presentation when you keep your hands behind your back while speaking. This can convey that you have something to hide, and no one wants to be surprised or tempted to wonder if you have other intentions. This is not a magic trick or optical illusion, which means that there should be no 'sleight of hand'.

Here is another aspect that is worth noting. We call this the 'wedding party' or the 'fig leaf' as in Adam and Eve from the Bible. This is where your hands are crossed over your waist or private area, and it looks like you are trying to protect your family jewels with your hands. While it also looks timid, it's especially awkward when you decide to gesture from this position. We don't want our audience to get the wrong idea after all.

Now, you may be thinking, "Then, how should I stand and what can I do with my arms?" How should you stand? What should your posture look like? Stand up and now imagine that you are a strong tree, with deep roots in the ground. Consider that a plant's root system can be just as broad and elaborate as the branches or what you see above the soil. This design is to provide stability and ensure greater access to water and nutrients. Your foundation much like that plant comes from your posture and positioning of your feet. Your feet should be hip-width apart. Relax your arms and let them be 'neutral' and hang loosely on your sides. This is a solid base position or posture. And it is where you should project yourself from while speaking. This is an acceptable position for the audience to receive your message. When in doubt about what to do with your hands, let them drop to your sides as this is your base position.

When using your hands and arms during your presentation, it is important to remember that the audience will respond to your movement - to your body language and that they can either be distracting or add value to your presentation. Proper usage of gestures can lend to your listeners remembering twice as much and imprint on their minds a fondness for wanting to hear from you again.

Strike One
We are huge sports fans and will periodically draw upon sports to make illustrations that our students may relate to. In the game of baseball, balls and strikes are determined solely by how the ball crosses the home plate and if that placement is within the 'strike zone[8]'. The strike zone is typically a box, ranging from the midpoint between a batter's shoulders and the top of the uniform pants -- when the batter is in his stance and prepared to swing at a pitched ball -- and a point just below the kneecap. Keep your gestures within the strike zone to avoid causing distraction and to increase the probability of a successful presentation.

Here are a few techniques that may be helpful for emphasis in certain aspects of your speech. These include the give or serve, the show, and the swing.

[16]

Talk It Up! - A Guide To Successful Public Speaking

Give Or Serve

This gesture is used to relay or provide facts- to essentially present something to your audience. The key with this gesture is to have the palms of your hands facing up and not down. Having your palms up will show that you have nothing to hide and that you are not withholding something from them. Graciously give and serve your audience. Let them receive the gift of your presentation. Next time you are watching a presentation, consider the posture and hand movement of the presenter. If the palms of their hands are facing up, you will likely comply or feel more comfortable with their message.

Uncross Those Arms

Don't cross your arms; this is a big no-no. When we communicate in this position, we convey disapproval, disappointment, and a whole slew of negative messages. What you want to say can be lost simply because you don't know what to do with your arms. You don't want to put your audience in an awkward position or leave them feeling insecure.

Instead, open yourself up by displaying or using a wide arms gesture. This is more inviting and shows your audience that you have nothing to hide. If you are at a loss and are not sure which position to have your arms, just drop them. Relax and drop them to your side and only use them when necessary to support your message.

A good rule of thumb is to never point at your audience. There are, however, exceptions to the rule. There may be moments where you need to make a strong point and invoke a sense of an urgency or even make clear that there is an emergency. Pointing can also come across as being bossy, and arrogant, and even make those you are addressing feel as if they are being reprimanded. Many of those in the profession of being politicians have even learned that it is better to use your thumb to make a 'point' instead of pointing.

Just remember that the gesture and the message must match, for example, you may say that sales and revenues have rapidly increased, but you use a downward chopping arm motion - this can depict the opposite. So, the next time you decide to use gestures, think about these three types and plan. The Gift, the Show, and the Chop.

To recap, your hand usage or gestures should reinforce your message. They should not be perceived as a threat, nor should they serve as a distraction. Remember that your body language can even convey nervousness, so be mindful and aware of your body language. Gestures work and that is the essential message.

Frequently, check the temperature of the room. Are they engaged? Don't be afraid of using a pattern disruption. For example, if they are seemingly losing focus, ask a question or ask for a volunteer to recap that section, etc.

[17]

Talk It Up! - A Guide To Successful Public Speaking

Walk With Confidence

I (David) teach a course on Executive Presence. We not only cover what executive presence is but that at the very core, we need to address our mindset. Our father used to challenge us to not only sit up straight but to also stand up straight. He said that this would also help with our confidence and help to make others confident in us.

Posture breeds success. First impressions matter and one is formed even before you take the stage to speak. It's important to know that your posture can either support or hurt your message. We have all seen both good and poor examples of this with presenters. You should never turn your back on the audience. Speakers can make the mistake of doing this to look at or read from their slide presentation or visual. This conveys a lack of confidence and does not help you to connect with your audience. Turning your back also communicates a lack of interest.

It's important, not just to know where to stand or speak from, but also how not to stand. Here are a few positions that we've seen that are not necessarily the best use of your body. The first is a no-no. Do not be that speaker who cannot help but keep their hands in their pockets. This comes across to your listeners as being nonchalant and it's very difficult to be convincing from this position.

Nonverbal communication can be highly effective if you can become highly aware of your body and even more so, your emotions. Do not take for granted how your feelings can affect your nonverbal communication. Try to become aware or in tune with your actions when you are tired, hungry, frustrated, anxious, and happy. Developing self-awareness can give you a greater mastery or control of your nonverbal communication.

Plan your nonverbal communication within your overall presentation and you will find greater success. We teach workshops on how to gain agreement and close more opportunities. In one of the workshops, we talk about the simple, yet effective use of nodding your head to gain buy-in or agreement. If you can get the audience to nod in agreement, then you have won or guided them toward a position of acceptance or approval. on

---

Visual Communication

Visual communication is the ability to present information with the use of images and mediums such as photography, art, maps, charts, and graphs. Visual communication can be a great avenue for those who are more visual learners and for adding that 'pop' to a presentation or speech. Do not underestimate the impact that can be made with the use of color, font, and sizes. Visual aids can help a speaker remember important topics, give the audience something to look at, and generally help convey the message being presented.

Visual communication is where the presenter uses images and media such as photography, art, maps, charts, and graphs. Visuals can be used to enhance a presentation by providing helpful context to the message being delivered. You will want to blend your visual aids into your presentation. Remember, that you never want your presentation to be just a slideshow. Always consider your audience and what would be appropriate. For more information on the role of technology and how to effectively use slides, we will dive into greater detail in Chapter 10: To Tech Or Not To Tech.

Because of advancements in technology, we now live, work, play - and interact in a world where visual communication including social media platforms such as Twitter, Instagram, Facebook, and LinkedIn posts with interactive experiences - is now the norm. We need to adapt and develop our communication skills.

Research Into The Forms Of Communication
Incredible research has been conducted on the role of personal communication. Mehrabian's 7-38-55 Rule[9] has shown that of these three: Words Spoken, Tonality, and Body language; that body language is by far the most effective. Tone (your voice) was at 38%, Verbal (words used) was at 7% and Body language (Visual) was at 55%. All three must be in harmony for a presenter to be fully effective. You must have a balance and so plan wisely to present the very best message in the most effective and impactful way.

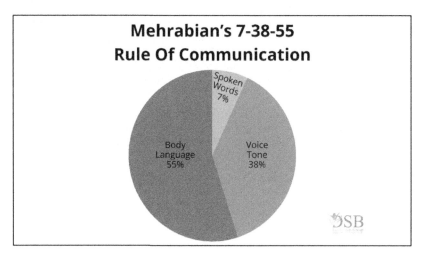

Reflection

So much information can be gathered from every interaction. What will the audience learn about you and from you when you speak? Understanding how to effectively use these forms of communication will greatly support your platform and increase your influence. Listening is impacted not only by the words you use but also by your body language and the tone of your voice. Decide to step outside of your comfort zone and step into opportunities for expanding your communication skills.

CHAPTER 3
Main Aspects Of Public Speaking

Public speaking is something that we all do every day. Everything from phone calls to team meetings presents opportunities to speak in public. What should the goal be with each interaction? What are you hoping will be accomplished or established? We want our clients and those who work with us to experience confidence and growth in being able to use their voices to increase their influence and value.

Before we go any further, we believe understanding key aspects of speaking to be necessary for establishing any expectations of becoming an effective speaker. While there could be many, we have determined the following four to be essential, and thus our four main aspects of public speaking.

1. The *Audience* - It's Not About You
2. The *Identity* (Speaker)
3. The *Message*
4. The *Setting*

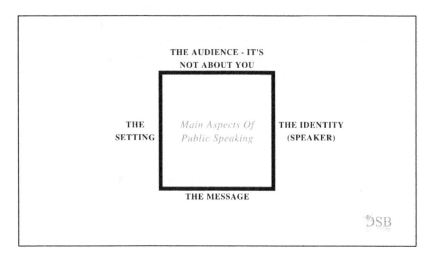

Look at the main aspects of speaking from a simple shape; that of a square, with the four sides being: the audience, the identity (speaker), the message, and the setting. Keep it simple and remember that for an effective message or presentation to take place, you must have all four of these sides firmly

Talk It Up! - A Guide To Successful Public Speaking

established. After you've grasped this, you will eventually get to the point in your own growth journey where you shatter your own expectations.

What is your subject? What are you passionate about? What are you the subject matter expert in? Let this excitement and energy fuel you and your speech. If you aren't excited about your message and your topic, then do not expect your audience to get excited about you, your message, or your topic.

If you are not a subject matter expert, then do yourself and your audience a favor by learning and growing in your own understanding of the material and area in which you will be speaking. The more you grow in your understanding and can grasp the material, the more you will become enthusiastic about the presentation. After all, who doesn't enjoy speaking freely about something they are passionate about.

---

1. The Audience - It's Not About You

Here is the key: It's not about you. Yes, we will briefly touch on the importance of how you see yourself and why it is of the utmost importance that you have the proper mindset before you even take the stage. This section is to help you grasp the value of taking the attention from you and placing that on those who will receive you and your message.

You have been given 'the stage' and their time and attention; now you must capture and keep it. Now what you do with that is what will determine your success. Audience and eye contact create credibility and connection. Quit looking at your notes and not your audience. Know your introduction. It takes seven seconds to make an impression and less than a second for the audience to decide if they will trust you.

Believe it or not, your audience wants you to be successful. They don't want this to be a waste of their time. Time is money and they could be doing something else. But they are not, they are there waiting for you. You have something to say, and they need to hear it. You may be the perfect subject matter expert, the perfect presenter for that group.

It's not about you. Make the audience your priority. Be your authentic self and connect with your audience and don't treat them as a task or tick off your checklist. Be with them in every aspect from your research to how you approach the stage or platform with your intention and your energy. We want you to visualize the spotlight being taken from you and putting it on your audience. It should not matter if you are speaking to an audience of five or an audience of 5,000. What is your audience looking for? Who are they and what are they concerned about? What will inspire them?

[22]

What is critical as a presenter is to know your audience. How much knowledge do they have about your subject; what you are representing? The more you know about your audience, the more likely you will be able to find success and exceed expectations. What does the audience need from you? Then consider the demographics of your audience including profession, age ranges, and culture if this is relevant. The more passionate you become about your topic, the more emotionally involved and tuned in you will become.

Committed
They are there, committed to you, and ready to be captivated by your message. You now need to be committed to them. You have been empowered with their time and attention. There is now no turning back. The first impression is always important and could be the most memorable one.

Start with a smile. There is something about a smile that is disarming and welcoming. Eye contact means connectivity. Can your gaze make them feel as if you are only speaking to them? Keep in mind that you don't want to stare or appear to be staring to the point where it could make someone feel uncomfortable.

Your audience is a partner to your success and in your discussion. Talk in terms of their interest.

We want you to consider the impact that will be made on your friends. Remember to view the audience as friends rather than strangers. Consider greeting and meeting the guests before you speak. This will lend the audience a feeling of both comfort and familiarity. Believe that they want you to succeed as much as you do. Therefore, they are there. For a moment, think about a recent sporting event or show you attended. You likely heard an athlete or a performer say that their performance was as good as it was because they were either in a zone or because of the audience or fans that were in attendance. How did they feed off this? Much like the athlete or performer, you also can feed off your audience and in turn feed them.

A great speaker will always do their homework and research their audience. It's all about demographics. Know the educational and professional background of those you will be presented to. Ages and socioeconomic background are of importance as well. What else do you think would be important to know? Reach out to the event organizer or event planner for any other information that may aid your presentation. Make a note of these as you adapt your message to increase the probability of having the most impact.

There's a saying that if you want to understand someone, then walk a mile in their shoes. Why would you want to do that? Why would you want to understand what someone has been through and how someone would feel about

[23]

a particular topic that is being presented? We want relatability; we want connectivity.

In every tear-jerking moment in filmmaking, the director has a goal to move the movie viewer emotionally. This could translate into the movie viewer feeling a depth of connectivity and sympathy with the characters on screen, that they cannot help but feel emotional. The best speakers have an incredible talent and gift for connecting at the 'heart level' with their audiences. We want them to walk away feeling as if the speaker "got me, understood me".

If you can genuinely hold to the thought that it's not about you, then you are already 'ahead of the game' and on your way to delivering an incredible presentation.

Engage
Don't just spit out information when they could simply do an online search or visit their local library. Don't read directly from your slides as they might be better served downloading the slide deck. Engage with them by connecting with them. If possible and according to your speaker style, you may want to somehow involve them. Audience participation can take place in different ways. What are some ways you can include your audience when speaking?

This helps to drive participation, increase attentiveness, and ultimately retention. The best way to get your audience excited about you and your presentation, and to stay involved, is to show up early. That's right, show up early to the event/venue and say hello.

If you've done a thorough job in your research, you will be able to craft well-timed questions or scenarios where audience participation will prove to make your presentation a home run. A well-timed/well-placed question can lead to a deeper commitment and increased attention

Although not something we like to use, you could ask the audience to raise their hands. You can ask them to try an exercise, to take out their cell phones, or to even ask for a volunteer. Be cautious with this one, especially if you have not asked them for help prior to your presentation, nor provided them with some direction.

The more you are able to involve the audience and turn the presentation into a conversation, the more emotionally involved they will become. It is annoying and a pet peeve to see a speaker ask the audience to clap their hands or to do 'the wave'.

Early in my (David) ministry career, I had a colleague on staff who on one particular Sunday morning was tasked with leading the 'Welcome Message'. He did something that apparently, he thought would be an 'awesome thing' to do.

Talk It Up! - A Guide To Successful Public Speaking

He may have picked up what he was about to do from attending an 'American' MLB Baseball game. He began by asking for all those attending the service to do the wave and an elderly lady in the front row attempted to stand up and sit down. It was embarrassing, and he learned a valuable lesson that there are more creative and even less 'physical' ways to engage with an audience.

The Power Of Storytelling

We dedicate the entirety of Chapter 9 to Storytelling, but for now, we want to point out that stories can be a powerful and effective tool. Stories can be an incredible method for engaging your audience. Knowing the demographics will lend insight for choosing that perfect story.

Find ways to engage with them. Realize that you have something to say and what you have to say can bring incredible value. Remember you are there to graciously give and serve your audience.

Energy

Energy, energy, energy. We cannot say enough about this one. Energy is contagious and can be like a wildfire gaining more energy with every flutter of wind from the audience. We are not asking for you to be the most excitable person in the room, but you better give off the vibe that you are excited and honored to be there. If the speaker is energetic, chances are that the audience will be more alert and even energetic. An energetic speaker can be infectious, pouring joy into the audience, while creating excitement and anticipation. Also, note that you should not be at the same energy level throughout the entire presentation. We are not in a group cycling class and I don't want to feel emotionally exhausted trying to keep up with your energy. Don't drink the espresso before you speak if you know that caffeine drives you to speak faster or to move more quickly than you need to - at least not for the duration of your presentation.

Energy can also be reflected by and affect the volume of your voice and the inflection that you are using, your eye contact, and movement of your body, especially of the arms. The last aspect of energy we will share is how you respond to the audience. It can be circular and if not careful, it can be damaging - where there is a lack of energy and response can lead a speaker to withdraw and get away from their objective. Your energy, passion, and enthusiasm will become a magnet and attract their masses. So, ask yourself the next time you speak if your audience matched your energy level. They will follow your lead. If you are not excited or fail to show excitement about your topic, then they will naturally lose excitement.

We will also cover an aspect of energy in Chapter 5, when we discuss speaking anxiety. Energy is amazing, as you can feed off the audience as much as they can feed off of you. This can be a healthy and encouraging aspect of energy.

[25]

Talk It Up! - A Guide To Successful Public Speaking

Remember that it is not about you - the more you learn about them, what they would want, the better your chance to knock it out of the park.

---

2. The Identity (Speaker)

Who are you? Not what everyone else says or even thinks about you, but what you think about yourself is what really matters. The key is to know deep inside what you believe about yourself. How you see yourself is of utmost importance as you can only control what you think of yourself.

Now I (David) do not currently have a $Million retainer policy like some of the most recognized leaders in the industry, but whenever I take the stage, I believe that I am the best speaker for that event. Why? You have to believe it or why would you take the stage? Why couldn't it be you? This is perhaps the most important question and factor in becoming that confident and effective speaker. You are the only one who can deliver that message in the way you can. The audience needs to hear from you; they need your voice.

There is only one of you! As identical twins, we know this all too well but also accept that it can be easy for others to 'place' you in a 'box'. We had decided that we were going to be known for who we were as individuals and not just as twins. There is only one David Suk Brown and only one Danny Suk Brown. We have similar passions and yet, we accept that we are unique and have different strengths. For example, I (Danny) typically handle any speaking engagements around the technology space.

What separates the very best athletes from their competitors? The margin may be razor-thin, but that edge may make the difference as far as who wins and who loses. We believe that what separates these elite athletes from others has more to do with their mindset than their talent. There is a resolve and a mental toughness that enables them to pull away and compete with the mindset of accepting nothing but winning.

The one thing we emphasize is that you must be your biggest advocate. Whenever you are tempted to feel as if no one is rooting for you, be reminded that you are your best cheerleader. We will talk about your message momentarily but note that your message reflects who you are. Your message reflects your brand and your speaking style. So, ask yourself, what gets you excited each day? What is your Why?

We have taught workshops on personal as well as organizational core values. These guide you and your actions. This along with our Speaker SWOT (Strengths, Weaknesses, Opportunities, Threats) Analysis will not only help you to identify your speaking strengths, but it can also help you to identify your

[26]

speaking voice and style. We've included a SWOT analysis in the bonus section of this book for you to work through.

When we were growing up, our parents knew that we each brought something different to the table, and yet, they emphasized working together in harmony. They taught us to notice our own strengths. This is why it is so vital that you lean on your distinctive strengths and learn what your own style is.

Vulnerability
We also want to address the incredible impact and power of vulnerability. Be authentic. This is where you are willing to be real and not come across as someone who is unrelatable. The last thing you want as a speaker is to come across as 'the emperor with new clothes'. Being vulnerable will help the audience feel for you. They want to help you - to in a way save you even though you are there too, in a sense, save them. When they hear your heart and potential hardship, they will stand with you and support you. They want you to be successful, they want their time with you to have been 'worth it'.

Style
What is your unique speaking style? We all have one. A speaker who is brewing with confidence doesn't sound like any other speaker. When training on this topic, our clients watch/listen to each other to only realize that a message or topic can be communicated effectively in many ways.

Some of us are very comfortable with storytelling. This is not necessarily a strength of David's, but it is one of mine (Danny). You will see later in this guidebook where I state that you should consider never making a point without a story and never sharing a story without making a point. So many are natural at this while others need to learn more about this art and skill.

A. The Motivator
When you think about the best motivational speakers, you might include names like Tony Robbins, Eric (ET) Thomas, Nick Vujicic, and Les Brown. You may also think about a friend, colleague, or another leader who all have 'that gift'. They are the ones who could 'sell ice to an Eskimo' and talk you into doing anything. They are the definition of a great car salesman. What is it about them that can make you feel a certain way - that can make you feel as if you could do anything without fail? Is it their energy, the strength of their voice, or charisma?

Perhaps you see yourself more as a motivational or inspirational speaker. You find joy in being able to inspire and lift others up. You are not only the 'glass is half full' leader or friend, but you are also the person holding the 'bottomless' pitcher with a smile on your face. You see the silver lining and find beauty when no one else does. This is your natural speaking style and the very best can

[27]

Talk It Up! - A Guide To Successful Public Speaking

leave you feeling a sense of hope in the darkest of moments. Lean in if this is your style as we need more and more of these speakers.

B.   The Entertainer
Who is your favorite entertainer? Who comes to mind first when you think about who the best comedian is? What about your favorite singer? This style works well to break up or change 'the mood'. The entertainer can often be characterized as someone who is animated and has endless use of facial expressions, and high energy. Keep in mind that we are not saying that you need to be great at telling jokes or become the master of one-liners.

Entertainers are often concerned with making sure those they are addressing are having a great time. You could be that entertainer.

C.   The Commander
This is the person who has to get the message across in a way that conveys seriousness and an urgency to get the job done. A characteristic of a commander is someone who gets to the point, speaks with intention, and usually has no problem with 'commanding' the room.

Those with this style are well prepared to deliver challenging news and can speak on issues that are especially sensitive or of grave importance. Which speakers come to mind when you think of commanders? Perhaps a school principal, a member of the military, or even an organizational leader.

D.   The Statistician
This style is very comfortable with statistics and facts. They use numbers to enhance their message. When thinking of those with this style, we often consider professors and teachers to reflect this more than most other professions.

What other styles are out there that should be noted? What is your style? You can learn from all these styles and even move within each of them by understanding how effective body language and voice inflection could be.

Be yourself, don't try to be somebody else. Find your own 'batting stance'. This is an illustration from baseball we often share in our training. Not all the players enter the batter's box with the same stance. They enter with a stance that they are most comfortable with. For those of us that love the sport, we may struggle with the length of the game and all the rituals and habits that these incredible athletes go through; but we appreciate that whatever their stance, it works for them, and we need them to be comfortable and confident to be at their best and to perform to the level of expecting a win. Go Cardinals - yes, we are St. Louis Cardinals fans.

[28]

Talk It Up! - A Guide To Successful Public Speaking

Batting Stance[1]

We often speak about finding your own speaker style as a baseball player finds their own batting style. Not all hitters use the same style as styles are born for comfort and confidence. Their batting stance provides them with the right mindset - one that will align with their vision for getting on base, advancing the runner, and ultimately helping the team to win. When starting to learn the sport, they often are taught the same foundational stance. As they grow and as their body matures, they adjust their stance.

You must find your own style and your own voice. You must discover what will work best for you.

---

3. The Message
Ethos, Pathos & Logos

Recall from Chapter 1 where Aristotle's components for persuasive speaking were covered.

Ethos, Pathos, and Logos are modes of persuasion used to convince and appeal to an audience. You need these qualities for your audience to accept your messages.

- **Ethos:** your credibility and character
- **Pathos:** emotional bond with your listeners
- **Logos:** logical and rational argument

Delivery & Momentum

Keep the momentum building as you work through your presentation. Build or transition from point to point. Try thinking of this as climbing a staircase. Build on what came before until the entire picture can be conveyed and grasped by the audience. This is where you zoom out until the whole picture can be seen clearly. Keep it as a conversation and not so rigid.

The Power Of A Pause

Do not downplay the significance of silence. Better to use a well-placed pause than to distract and irritate your audience with 'ums' and 'you knows'. A pause can draw an audience in and have them wanting to know what you will be sharing next. Each time you pause, you can draw their attention back to you. A pause can also allow time for the audience to soak in the point or illustration you just provided.

Talk It Up! - A Guide To Successful Public Speaking

Consider these examples:

- A speaker could state, "Here is the key to making six figures this week". Now the speaker pauses. Be silent as the audience ponders how 'six figures could be made'. The silence builds anticipation.
- A speaker mentions ever so calmly that it is time to "reveal the secret ingredient to the recipe that has won the title of best chef seven years in a row". Now is the time to place a pause because. This audience also cannot wait to learn what the secret ingredient is.

Another way to use a pause and draw the audience is to ask for audience participation without asking. For instance, you could start a quote or place a well-timed saying that everyone knows and then pause for them to finish the quote or saying. Here is an example: 'what goes up' (now pause). They will say 'must come down'. Here's another example: 'Winning isn't everything'. The audience will finish the quote by saying, 'it's the only thing'. Let's try another one: 'fool me once, shame on you', 'fool me twice, (then pause) 'shame on me'.

A pause can also be for you and not just the audience. This is especially true for those who speak very quickly. Breathe. It is also helpful for transitions or even remembering where you are and where you need to go next with your presentation.

---

4. Setting
Watch any survival program and you will quickly be reminded of how important it is to be familiar with your surroundings as this can mean life or death. Having knowledge of your settings before you speak could mean success or failure.

We do a deeper dive into this later in the guidebook, but for the moment, here are a few things you should know.
Is there an event planner or event organizer? They are your first and best resource for understanding the setting - for understanding what you will be facing before and while you are speaking.

What is the layout of the room? How big is the stage or area from which you will be presenting? What type of technology will be in use, and will it be compatible with your technology (if you are using any)? Take a note of the lighting and sound as well. Is there a wireless (aka lavalier) handheld or stationary mic? Can you send your presentation over before the event to ensure no issues?

[30]

Talk It Up! - A Guide To Successful Public Speaking

Time Management
Speakers often fail to realize the importance of time management. Often, they don't realize the amount of content they will deliver should be carefully considered to match their allotted speaking time.

Make it a priority to include practicing your presentation several times to gauge your handle on time. Factor in audience involvement/engagement - or times you may need to open your presentation for audience participation/interaction.

Is there a timer/clock? Unless you've given a specific speech 'hundreds of times', it can be a challenge to keep an eye on your time. Often venues and larger events will provide a countdown clock of some type. The timer may or may not include a lighting system (green, yellow, and red). If there are no timers/clock down clocks, then ask the event organizer to hold a card, poster or monitor of some type to signal the amount of time you have remaining (for example "five minutes" or "one minute").

It's better by far to finish early than to convey a sense of needing to 'dump' or 'cram' information, to cross that proverbial 'finish line', only to not provide space or time for any feedback or questions.

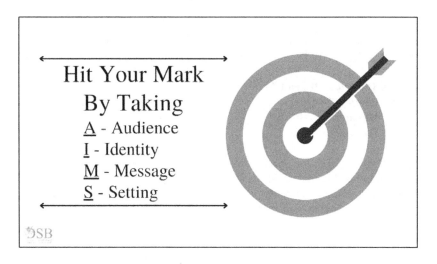

Hit Your Mark By Taking AIMS
We looked at the four main aspects of speaking.

1. The *Audience* - It's Not About You
2. The *Identity* (Speaker)
3. The *Message*
4. The *Setting*

Talk It Up! - A Guide To Successful Public Speaking

Once you've grasped these four aspects, you simply need only to take AIM(S) and hit your target. Hitting your goal is a matter of understanding these four aspects of speaking. If you want to hit the mark; then make sure your AIM is true. This comes from practice and understanding certain concepts (like archery).

There is a quote that is often attributed to the great Hockey icon Wayne Gretzky where he states, "You miss 100% of the shots you don't take[2]". This expression is also common in other sports including basketball and baseball: "You can't score if you don't shoot" and "You can hit the ball if you don't swing". Wayne Gretzky was essentially saying that you cannot succeed if you don't try. Your belief must lead to action.

Your belief in yourself will propel you toward becoming the speaker you know you can and should be. There is only one you.

Reflection
This might be difficult to swallow, but remember, that this is not about you. This is about your audience. They are invested in your success as they are there for a reason. This alone removes some of the pressure to perform and not make any 'mistakes'.

What's the best way to hit your target audience? Remember the acronym A.I.M.S. and you will hit your mark, no matter the perceived pressure. These are:
1. The *Audience* - It's Not About You
2. The *Identity* (Speaker)
3. The *Message*
4. The *Setting*

The parts of A.I.M.S. are specifically tailored to support a speaker looking to make that incredible impact. It is a template for providing clarity, ensuring that the audience is front and center as the focus. It is to prepare the presenter by providing focus so that their message connects. Use A.I.M.S. and that bullseye won't seem so far away.

[32]

CHAPTER 4
The Power Of Visualization

You've earned the right, so speak. Be excited to take the stage. If you aren't excited about what you are going to share, there is little chance of the audience being excited. Keep in mind that no one wants to hear from someone who comes across as boring and lacking enthusiasm.

You will notice throughout this guidebook the emphases we place on practice and preparation. You can practice something repeatedly with the goal of being able to perform or do that action without hesitation and to 'perfection'. This chapter is designed to encourage you to take your mindset to another level - one of certainty and conviction. That belief in yourself and of being certain of absolute success is what will lead you to fulfilling your true potential - and to your desired goal.

Before we get into what visualization is, we want to first encourage you to consider making this a habit. Something that you do so consistently that it becomes in a way like second nature or like muscle memory. I (Danny) often share with those I train about building healthy habits and setting your mind for success. There was a speech given to the graduating class of the University of Texas at Austin in 2014[1] and then a book by General William H. McRaven entitled *Make Your Bed: Little Things That Can Change Your Life...And Maybe the World*[2]. He shared principles he learned throughout his life and Naval Career, including his Navy Seals training. He believed that anyone could take these principles to change the world.

In it, McRaven says "Life is a struggle and the potential for failure is ever-present, but those who live in fear of failure or hardship, or embarrassment will never achieve their potential. Without pushing your limits, without occasionally sliding down the rope headfirst, without daring greatly, you will never know what is truly possible in your life.[2]" How can you not be inspired? And what is just as amazing as hearing this speech or reading these words is what he shared about simple habits - starting with that of making your bed. That accomplishment will give you a "small sense of pride and will encourage you to do another task; and another. That action will reinforce the fact that little things matter...If you want to change the world, start off by making your bed.[3]"

This habit is building what success is. Building your mind is much the same. Practicing visualization is in many ways much like the mental habit of 'making your bed'. What is visualization? It is a technique and tool. This is a practice of

Talk It Up! - A Guide To Successful Public Speaking

strengthening, shaping, and affirming the mind through mental imagery. We are going to shape or channel self-image.

Through the exercise or practice of visualization, you will see yourself accomplishing your goals. So set your mind for success. You have earned the right to speak. Your actions will align with the benefits that come from accomplishing your goals.

We all have unconscious beliefs (in the subconscious mind) about ourselves and about our speaking abilities. Do you have any limiting beliefs about your speaking? Imagine what would happen if we took the time to dispel those limiting and inaccurate beliefs? Imagine if we replaced those limiting beliefs with real actionable experiences and transformed our thinking. The practice of visualization allows for reality to come closer to that image. Let us be deliberate with shaping our subconscious minds and attain our goals and objectives. Visualization is a vehicle for obtaining that.

When I (David) was in High School, I wanted to run as fast as my twin. Danny was on the track team and was one of the fastest athletes in the school. I knew that I was fast, but I remember thinking that I could never beat him. I would think this every time we lined up to run. By now, you likely know the outcome of those races. I did not overcome my twin because, in my mind, I could not overcome my limiting belief. After being frustrated enough times, I decided to try something different. I had heard that for professional athletes what separated the 'best from the rest' was not talent but the mindset. Could I beat him if I first won in my mind? Yes, I could, and I would defeat my brother during the Freshman year of college.

I could not consistently overtake Danny in running but I was more than thrilled by the fact that I had won and was no longer going to be held back from crossing that finish line and breaking that tape. Break the tape with the power of visualization.

The same thing happened when I could never seem to run a mile under five minutes. I would come close and yet it seemed so far away.

The same thing happened again when I started swimming laps in the pool. I could not possibly swim for a mile nonstop. I learned to take control of my mind and my body and eventually got to the point where I could.

The same thing happened when I first started to speak before what some would consider a large crowd.

Reflect on a time during a sporting event, performance, project, or difficult decision you had to make. You likely thought through your event or activity using your imagination. You imagined how things would unfold. You began to

[34]

Talk It Up! - A Guide To Successful Public Speaking

feel a spirit of courage and resolve grow within you. This is the power of visualization. Before those events unfolded, did you picture everything that could go wrong? What about everything that could go right? There is great power when you choose to focus on what can go right instead.

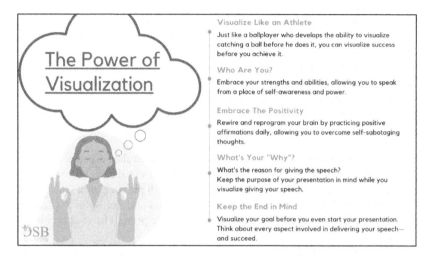

The Power of Visualization

Visualize Like an Athlete
Just like a ballplayer who develops the ability to visualize catching a ball before he does it, you can visualize success before you achieve it.

Who Are You?
Embrace your strengths and abilities, allowing you to speak from a place of self-awareness and power.

Embrace The Positivity
Rewire and reprogram your brain by practicing positive affirmations daily, allowing you to overcome self-sabotaging thoughts.

What's Your "Why"?
What's the reason for giving the speech? Keep the purpose of your presentation in mind while you visualize giving your speech.

Keep the End in Mind
Visualize your goal before you even start your presentation. Think about every aspect involved in delivering your speech— and succeed.

Tips For Visualization
A. Empower Yourself

There is a worksheet entitled 'Your Affirmation List'[4] (see bonus materials for this list.) that we would like for you to complete. This activity can lead to a paradigm shift). The Affirmation exercise will aid you in embracing your strengths and ability to speak because you will start from a place of strength and self-awareness. Reminding yourself daily will build your confidence and reshape your self-image.

I (David) audited a class at Johns Hopkins University on Positive Psychology. The professor shared about the ability to reprogram or should I say rewire the brain. Everything from consistently using a 'gratitude journal', reading to believing Affirmation Statements, and implementing visualization can go a long way to attaining this.[5]

There is incredible power in knowing who you are. There is freedom with clarity. Be clear with your expectations and then break any negative belief system. Plant that expectation like a seed and your commitment to watering and caring will sprout and grow into reality. The key is to be clear with your expectations. What is it you really want?

B. Schedule An Appointment With Yourself

It is very difficult to pour into others without first pouring into yourself. For this to become a habit and produce desired results, you need to be committed to this practice. Schedule it for the same time every day (even several times

Talk It Up! - A Guide To Successful Public Speaking

throughout the day) and make sure it is in a quiet place. You are going to need at least 5-15 minutes. We also recommend that you close your eyes to maximize the experience.

C. Visualize Your Goal

You are there for a reason, so set a focus for your visualization. Be as specific as you can about your goal. Thinking about why you are speaking will take some of the pressure off what you may be tempted to feel. Think about the impact and difference that will be made because of your presentation. Think about what the audience will leave with. They will not only see your passion - they will also feel it. Don't focus on getting something from the audience or from your boss or your coworkers. Focus rather on what you can give the audience.

Throughout this exercise, it is important that you are relaxed and learning to control your breathing. More on breathing techniques in the section where we touch on overcoming speaking anxiety. With enough practice, you will also be able to calm and center your mind enough to focus and not be overwhelmed with everything that can come across your mind. Be present in your mind.

The key is to be as vivid and as detailed as possible. We will discuss that more in the next step.

D. Visualize The Setting

As you grow in this exercise, you may even grow in your ability to tie in your other senses. You will start to imagine how everything will sound, smell, and feel. What does it sound like and feel like to be on that stage?

During this exercise, you will consider the venue, the lighting, sound, technology, and the audience. Ask how large the stage is and how far from the audience you will be when you present. What is your proximity to the audience? How much movement will there be? Do you know how to get on and off the stage? Lighting is crucial and can impact your use of or decision to use technology and visual aids. I would highly encourage you to arrive at the venue you will be presenting at early - if not the day before. Become familiar with the place, the setting, and the technology (microphone - wireless or handheld and check to ensure your presentation slides or PowerPoint work). If you are alone, you can even have a walkthrough of your presentation.

E. Visualize Your Speech

Think about your mission - about your why. What do you want the audience to walk away from their time with you? Do you want them to change something or to learn something? Do you want them to be inspired or convicted? Visualize yourself giving your speech or presentation. Consider your speaking style, voice level, and fluctuations and then finally the successful completion of the speech itself.

[36]

Talk It Up! - A Guide To Successful Public Speaking

F. Visualize Your Emotion Which Is Born From Your Action - Your Energy

This is your energy in motion. When you are attaching emotion or feeling strong enough to your exercise of visualization, this is when those goals come to life. Out of those emotions and strong feelings, you will see the fruit of action. Those images are not just images but a foretelling of what will happen.

Try visualizing your introduction. Say it out loud and now close your eyes and 'see' yourself delivering that powerful introduction. Do it repeatedly and see the emotion and energy with your eyes closed. Now open them.

The more real this seems and feels to you, the better. We are going from the conscious mind to the subconscious mind, which then begins to program or reprogram itself.

Try
- Raise your right arm up parallel to your shoulder and the ground. Rotate that right arm to the right as far as you can go. Now, close your eyes and without physically doing anything, imagine your outstretched arm rotating even further. Picture this repeatedly and attach a strong emotion such as joy or a feeling of victory. Now open your eyes and do the same thing again. You will discover yourself going beyond what you had initially tried.
- Clasp your hands together. Which thumb is on top? You don't think about it, but your mind and body 'naturally' gravitate to this same thumb being on top. It might feel a bit awkward if you now try to clasp your hands together with the opposite thumb on top. However, by consciously placing your other thumb on top, you have just shifted a subconscious behavior and belief. The same can be said with how you put on your pants and with which leg you place in the pants first.

These may seem minor but for a speaker, these 'little shifts' can mean everything. This is the beauty of visualization.

The potential was there the entire time. Through the power of visualization, you were able to take action to get better results. The difference is a change of belief. Through the power of visualization, you were able to see your desired result You saw it, felt it, and believed it. Your belief system changed. Remember that the subconscious mind is programmed or reprogrammed through repetition and with strong Emotion attached through visualization.

Consider when athletes say that they are in the zone. This is where things seem to slow down.

[37]

Talk It Up! - A Guide To Successful Public Speaking

Activity

1. *Complete* the 'Your Affirmation List[4]' in the 'Workshop' section of this book.

2. *Take* a moment before you start your day with a simple visualization exercise. Relax your breathing and close your eyes. Think about what your day will look like. Consider your interactions, the experiences, and the emotions that might feel. Take it all in. If you are speaking, think about the venue and even what you will be wearing. Visualize the win. Then open your eyes and go attack the day.

CHAPTER 5
Dealing With Speaking Anxiety A.K.A. Nerves

Do you suddenly get stage fright or draw a blank just before you are about to speak? Have you ever felt as if you were becoming lightheaded, noticed your body temperature increasing or your hands begin to moisten? You are not unique in your fear of public speaking. There have been studies that reflect this. Up to 90% of those who participate in speech classes often state that they began because of their fear of speaking, and not simply to polish up their speaking skills. Many of them find that working on their speaking skills has even helped them to overcome other insecurities.

Don't buy the lie that the great presenters never get nervous. I once heard someone say, 'if you don't get nervous, you are lying'. You are not alone, even the both of us get nervous. It's about managing those nerves.

Now that we've established that nerves can affect even the best of us, we have to ask why we are so afraid of speaking? According to studies, glossophobia, also known as the fear of speaking, is America's biggest phobia followed by the fear of heights and the fear of bugs. According to a study by Chapman University, there are more people (25.3%) afraid of speaking than there are who are afraid of clowns (7.6%)[1]. Have they not seen the movie IT? While fear itself is rooted in the perception of harm, experiences or the lack thereof play a major factor.

We want to address what we have found to be the real culprit behind the fear of speaking. You might just be afraid of being judged. When you accept this, the fear of speaking will no longer grip or paralyze you. Let's pause here for a moment. We do not have medical degrees or a background in psychology. We do not for a moment believe that we fully understand social anxiety disorders. We embrace the balance and overall health of our clients, and strongly encourage medical assistance for those who believe this could be more than a feeling of shyness or anxiousness. There may come a time when a motivational talk is not enough to get you to where you want to be as a speaker. Let's work together with leading medical and mental health experts to support your personal and professional goals.

Many of us want to be liked and accepted and rejection strikes the heart of our fears. We can become uncomfortable with being the focus of every person in the room. The key is not to think that you will never become nervous or that

Talk It Up! - A Guide To Successful Public Speaking

you must become 'fearless' to take the stage. You must increase your awareness and gain more control over your fear, whether that fear is real or imagined.

Don't buy into the 'see your audience as naked or see them in their undergarments'. This does not truly help you as a presenter. The last thing you want your audience to feel is uncomfortable because of the way you look at them. This odd advice only seems to present more complications. Imagine me (David) as a minister training other ministers to imagine their congregation members as naked or in their undergarments whenever they spoke. There is a reason why we wear clothing.

A sense of or certain amount of 'stage fright' can be useful. Our instincts are there to protect us and can keep us alert and aware of our surroundings and actions. Use this to your advantage.

In a few moments, we will share techniques that may help you to accomplish your goal - your goal of delivering a successful presentation or speech. First, let's look at some possible signs of anxiety. See the signs, acknowledge them, and then move forward with the techniques and channel that nervousness into positive energy!

- *Sweaty hands*. There are those who naturally produce moisture in the palms of their hands even when the temperature isn't hot or raised above a certain degree, such as 70°F. We are talking about a sign of nerves. Sweaty hands in this instance can be a result of or a reaction to a strong emotional response. They can be triggered by feelings of fear and anxiety. This can be addressed with growth in confidence and management of your anxiety, with or without medical intervention.
- *Dry mouth aka frog in your throat*. Have you ever had a dry mouth? This could be a sign of anxiety and not just a medical or health condition. This can be very challenging when you are in a position where you have to present before your board of directors or upper management and leadership within your organization or even if you are looking for that next career change. Having a dry mouth could affect your ability to convey yourself as a confident leader. Consider using lip balm and look at your diet. You want to be and stay hydrated. Avoid caffeine, tobacco, alcohol, and even certain mouthwashes, especially when you know you will be speaking as these can cause dehydration. Keep room temperature water handy. You can also try gum or mints but please do not forget to get rid of them before you speak. Speak with your doctor as there may be treatments or medication such as artificial saliva that can help.
- *Swallow your words.* Swallowing your words could literally mean swallowing your words as you're speaking. This is very obvious to people, and you could come across not only as someone who is nervous but also as somebody who's also not competent or credible.

Talk It Up! - A Guide To Successful Public Speaking

- *You could also say the opposite is true.* Too much saliva can affect your performance as well. Do people ask, 'what about when I have to swallow while I speak'? This definitely could be a sign of nervousness, but this could be an opportunity for you to implement the power of the pause (will cover this shortly). If you have control over your body and understand the power of body language you do not have to be overly dramatic about swallowing.
- *Speaking fast.* Do you find yourself speaking rather quickly? You are not in high school on the debate team, nor are you, we assume, a voice-over actor who is being paid to speak a '100 miles per hour' as if you are speaking at the end of every commercial.
- *Butterflies in the stomach.* Ever felt those butterflies?
- *Rapid heartbeat.* Why does it feel like your heart is about to burst out of your chest? The pace of your breathing has increased, and you are starting to wonder if you even know how to breathe.

Techniques

We all get nervous, and we may or may not have coping mechanisms to help us through those times. Could you implement those same techniques when it comes to handling nerves with public speaking?

First, make a list of real versus perceived concerns. Accept facts and learn what is true and false about you and your situation. You cannot control what others choose to think about you or your presentation, so, let them stare and let them judge. This will not last 'forever' and chances are that the majority of those there will forget and become unaware of many aspects of the meeting. Those who see or interact with you on a consistent basis will draw more from their understanding of who they believe you are, in character and traits they have observed, rather than one incident. Your pattern of consistent behavior will weigh more favorably than any poor 'performance'.

Next, reflect on your belief system to avoid any self-defeating talk. This is not the time to play that broken 'tape' of how you are not good enough, as that is counter to how you need to see yourself. Take those fears and compare them with what you know to be true about yourself. Recall your affirmation statements and core values. Strengthen your case!

When you think about having to speak, what feelings come to mind? We touched upon some of the signs of fear: sweating, a racing heart, feelings of being judged, humiliated, rejected, and feelings of failure. What about success? Yes, success because if you are successful, this may mean you will be called upon more often to speak. Fear comes from uncertainty. Fear comes from not being in control. Wait a second. When you speak, you are the one in control. Replace the thought of "I have to" with "I get to". This is so freeing. Shift your

[41]

Talk It Up! - A Guide To Successful Public Speaking

perspective and that nervousness will become positive energy. Channel that potential fear and anxiety into high performance and impact. Channel it by being prepared and by focusing on your goal. Don't let speaking cripple you. Let the opportunity to speak free you.

Here is something that may be worth noting: you can replace those self-preservation habits with new positive habits and deliver with the full power of your vocal capacity. Next are some things you can try to help conquer your nerves.

Mindset
Appreciate who you are and acknowledge your decision to run toward and not away from this area of speaking. The fact is that you are courageous enough to improve this vital skill. You are choosing not to stay in a state of fear. This book is designed to help you not only become more poised and grow in your self-confidence, but you will also welcome more opportunities to speak and present.

- *Embrace* the importance of your role and why your audience needs to hear from you. Shift your focus from performance to communication and giving. A different cognitive approach includes shifting your perspective from being evaluated to being of value. You train yourself to see public speaking as a situation where you are communicating with people, something that you think they will benefit from, instead of thinking of it as a situation where you will be tested and judged. That shift in perspective relieves you of the worry of how you will come across and focuses you on how to best get your message across.
- *Expect success*! You will accomplish your goal.
- *Challenge your beliefs* about your ability to prepare and deliver an effective and impactful speech. Cognitive reframing approaches target your negative self-statements (I am not a good speaker; audiences find me boring), or any irrational beliefs about public speaking (People can see how anxious I am on stage). Irrational, in this case, means that your beliefs are not supported by the facts or by your experience. Cognitive reframing helps you challenge negative statements and beliefs and replace them with favorable, supportive, and proactive statements. It is important to note that these techniques are not intended to simply replace negative thinking with vapid and meaningless statements. They challenge you to think more pragmatically and intentionally. In essence, you are teaching yourself to see public speaking as a non-threatening event that you can learn to handle and to see yourself as a confident speaker-in-progress.
- *Challenge specific worries*. When there are uncertainties, you may overestimate the likelihood of bad things happening. List your specific worries. Then directly challenge them by identifying probable and

[42]

alternative outcomes and any objective evidence that could support each worry or the likelihood that those concerns will happen. Become familiar with the setting/venue, event schedule, and technology, so you are not surprised at the time of your presentation.

- **Visualize your success.** Imagine that your presentation will go well. Positive thoughts can help decrease some of your negativity about your social performance and relieve some anxiety. Mindfulness is a practice that could be integrated into your daily routine and not just before a presentation. We spoke about this in an earlier chapter.

- **Awareness.** Be Present. Being centered and aware of your emotional state can be beneficial.

- **Know your stuff.** Make sure you are knowledgeable about the subject. Become absorbed by your topic or subject. The more you focus on what you are going to present, the easier it will be to deliver that information or message with confidence. This cannot be overstated, know your topic. The better you understand what you're talking about — and the more you care about the topic — the less likely you'll make a mistake or get off track. And if you do get lost, you'll be able to recover quickly. Take some time to consider what questions the audience may ask and have your responses ready.

- **Organize.** Ahead of time, carefully plan out the information you want to present, including any props, audio, or visual aids. The more organized you are, the less nervous you'll be. Use an outline on a small card to stay on track. If possible, visit the place where you'll be speaking and review available equipment before your presentation.

- **Practice and prepare.** Set aside enough time to prepare and practice. A lack of preparation can be apparent. So set aside the appropriate time and stick to a process that works best for you. Practice will lead to increased confidence in yourself as you capture the benefits of repeating the right process. Never buy into the thought that you don't need to prepare and that you can wing it. We have all been there when we've heard a presentation like this. We feel cheated and not valued. If the presenter cared enough about the audience, they would have prepared. Your message may be the one they need to remember. In Chapters 6 & 7, we will revisit how preparation and the structure or outline of your presentation go a long way to setting yourself up for success.

- **Practice, and then practice some more.** Practice your complete presentation several times. Do it for some people you're comfortable with and ask for feedback. It may also be helpful to practice with a few people with whom you're less familiar. Consider making a video of your presentation so you can watch it and see opportunities for improvement.

- **Writing exercise.** Try a simple writing exercise with 2 columns (worksheet). What could happen if people acted or adopted the thinking you are going after? Compare that to what could happen if you do not present or speak with them. List past experiences of successful leadership and goals you have accomplished and how they made you feel. Don't get

[43]

caught up with what you might lose in speaking and be consumed with the passion you have and with the impact you will have on those who will hear you. Focus on your purpose. Also, please take some time to complete your Affirmation list and repeat this to yourself throughout the day. What you put into your mind will shape what you believe.

- *Meditation*. Meditation is a great tool, yoga is a great exercise, and both activities always start with proper breathing techniques. Focused breathing can do wonders for calming anxiety and for centering the mind. When you are nervous, you can 'forget to breathe' in that you don't' consider the power of controlled breathing to calm anxiety. You may also find yourself breathing quite rapidly. Your breathing may become shallow and speed up. This does not lend to the clarity of mind nor support the body or the mindset you need to have before taking the stage.
- *Breathe*. Breathing strategies and techniques that will support you in getting centered and grounded. These will help you to become present (sense of well-being) and help prepare you for social interactions including taking the stage.
- *Do* some deep breathing. Breathing exercises and techniques can reduce anxiety and enhance your speaking voice. Start with a straight posture, relax your body, focus on your abdomen while breathing in through your nose, and then exhaling through your mouth. Begin with three- or four-second intervals to ensure deeper instead of shallow breathing.

Additional Things To Consider
Begin with your posture by standing or sitting with your back straight. Beginning with your shoulders, relax your body to release any tension. You may want to close your eyes to aid in your concentration. Think about 'belly breathing' or the filling of your abdomen first and then up through your chest. You will know you are doing this technique if by breathing in, your stomach expands and now your chest as evidenced by your shoulders widening.

Gently breathe in through your nose for a four-second count, hold it in for 4 seconds and then exhale through your mouth for a 4-second count. We have seen others share this model with either a triangle shape or a square shape.

There are different breathing techniques, so it would be wise to take some time and discover what would work best for you. Once you do, practice and implement this as part of your daily routine.

Physical Exercise
There are many benefits that come from a daily exercise routine. A consistent exercise regimen can do wonders for your confidence and for gaining more control over your body. We can't state enough how cardio, and flexibility can lead to increased awareness. You may want to consult with your physician before any drastic changes you make to your exercise routine to ensure you

Talk It Up! - A Guide To Successful Public Speaking

properly 'build up' toward your desired goals. You don't want to hurt yourself in the process of trying to improve yourself.

Something You Can Try Now
Loosen your arms and wriggle your toes in a way to relax your body. Think of yourself being like a tree with deep roots and outstretched branches. You have now created a solid base and are able to 'extend' yourself to the audience.

Rest
Rest, sleep, and learning to relax are essential to a healthy mind and body. Without proper rest, you cannot expect peak performance; you cannot expect to function consistently at a high level.

Professional Support
Psychologists, hypnosis treatments, and speech coaches like myself. In our coaching practices, we let our clients know that we are not medical doctors and never want them to assume that our training and coaching is 'enough' nor should they ignore advice from their physician or medical doctor. There are times we will encourage medical support. We view this as working in concert or alongside and not instead of.

It is of the utmost importance that mental and physical health is factored first before anything else. We adjust to support our clients and want them to know that there may be a need to pause while they get the necessary help. There are also times when we implement mindfulness and mindset coaching to support their drive to grow in their effectiveness as a speaker. You can give someone all the tools but without the right mindset, they do little to promote lasting change and impact. Please refer to the section of the guidebook on affirmations and visualization or reach out to our company for more insight into our executive coaching.

'Be like Mike if I can be like Mike[2]'
While this is not everyone's 'cup of tea' or preferred approach; there are those who like to emulate what they see in many athletes. Many of their favorite athletes will 'psych' themselves up before their event, and they may even 'psych' themselves up during their event. They jump, give each other high-fives, and essentially do whatever it takes to get excited. Teammates at the office or on the field do this to celebrate and stay excited.

'The Power Of The Pause'
This is one of the phrases many of our students say is one of their most memorable from our training. The power of the pause can do so much to strengthen your credibility as a speaker. A well-placed pause will allow you a moment to center yourself and gather your thoughts. A well-placed pause will allow you a moment to 'find your place' and continue your presentation. A well-

[45]

Talk It Up! - A Guide To Successful Public Speaking

placed pause will allow your audience a moment to soak in and process what you've just shared.

Consider using the pause to welcome audience participation. This will increase attentiveness and even allow you that moment to swallow, collect yourself, and even smile. You got this, so remember the power of the pause.

Rely on your Inner Circle. Who do you trust to have your back when you need support and positive reinforcement? Invite these allies into your inner circle and accept only positive energy.

Coaching
We would not be trainers and coaches if we did not include a thought or two about the role of coaching to support you in overcoming speaking anxieties. Coaching should not be limited to that of a public speaking coach, but also to an executive or mindset coach. Mindset coaches help leaders remove mental barriers to their client's success.

Key
Our thought is that you should find what will work best for you and then implement it before you speak.

Reflection
1. *What* works best for you when you start to feel anxious or nervous?
2. *Can* you somehow tie this coping mechanism into managing any concerns around your speaking?
3. *Can* you revisit what nurturing a positive mindset looks like?

CHAPTER 6
Say It In A Sentence: Create & Structure

You've been asked to give a presentation at the next upcoming company quarterly meeting. This can be an incredible opportunity to not only share your thoughts but to extend your brand and influence. Between that invitation and the company meeting, you are repeatedly asked what your presentation will be about. What do you say? Can you sum it up and say it in a sentence? If you cannot say what your message will be about in a sentence or two, then it is likely too confusing or too complicated.

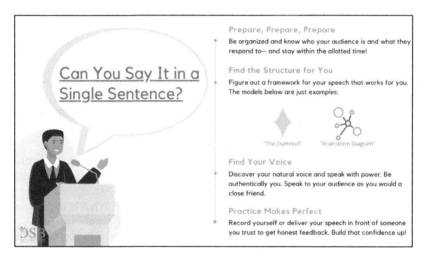

After we've established what the main aspects of speaking are, let's create your speech or presentation. Remember to stick as closely to those areas as possible to deliver a more concise and clear presentation. This is the formula for a strong and effective presentation.

Stephen Covey stated that you should begin with the end in mind[1]. Before you begin preparing that speech, you should begin with the audience in mind and what you expect them to take away from your message. How do you want them to think? What actions do you want from them? Remember that it is not about you! This will take the pressure and focus off yourself and back on what is most important.

Do your homework and learn the demographics of the audience. Speak with the event organizer or key personnel and learn as much as you can about your

Talk It Up! - A Guide To Successful Public Speaking

audience. The more you understand who you will be addressing, the greater the success. This understanding of your audience aids in the development of the right message.

We are often complimented by our podcast guests and our listeners for the depth of our content and for how we determine which questions to ask. While we were never trained in journalism, we believe that we are all born with the same spirit of curiosity. We want to discover ways of asking questions that others would never ask. We do our research and are spurred on by our curiosity to learn more about those we are interviewing.

You must be willing to do your research and learn more about your audience to craft and deliver the right message - a message that will resonate and remain.

Things To Learn About Your Audience

- *What* is the number of people who will expect to hear your message (in person and/or virtual)?
- *What* is the industry and lifestyle you will be addressing?
- *What* are the age ranges and levels of education?
- *Ask* why they are there to listen to you. What do they hope to get from their time with you?
- *Is* there a problem, concern, pain point, or issue that will speak directly to them?
- *What* if any cultural factors should you understand?
- *What* regional or cultural norms and perspectives should you be aware of? This will not only guide what you eventually prepare and present; it will also guide how you dress, speak, and interact with those in attendance.
- *What* do you want them to do with what you present? What is the action or thought that will be challenged and even changed by you?
- *Ask* how you can best connect and reach them. This will dictate your choice of visual aids and added materials.

Keep It Simple
As you go through this book, you will gather how important it is to be your authentic self when you speak. You will be with the mindset and through practice, more relatable and comfortable at conveying your message. Don't be overwhelmed and overthink this. This is where you must believe that 'less is more'. Keeping it simple will allow you to add 'meat to the bones' of your presentation. Therein lies the answer: keep it simple and you will find more opportunities to penetrate deeper within that angle or niche.

From time to time, we are asked what topics speakers should focus on. A great place to begin to understand the expectations and needs of the event organizer.

[48]

Talk It Up! - A Guide To Successful Public Speaking

The nature of the event itself could indicate what the topic should be centered on. Outside of topics being expected, they often wonder if they were given the freedom to choose a topic or area of focus, what might it be.

Ask yourself, what you are most passionate about. What would you be considered a subject matter expert in? What aligns with your core values and what would you easily be able to share with passion, excitement, and conviction? What topic would reflect your personality and speaking style? Personally, we have no problem deferring based on our own strengths and passions.

Once you've identified your topic or what you will be speaking about and have done your research into the audience you will be addressing, you will next develop the outline and presentation itself.

Speech Construction & Outline
Without structure, a speech can become a distraction, disinteresting, and even a disaster. You can easily organize your speech or presentation with the following formula in mind:

*1. **Tell** the audience what you are going to tell them.
*2. **Tell** them
*3. **Tell** them what you've told them (highlight benefits of the asked task)

Perhaps you have heard the adage "work smarter, not harder", or the acronym KISS which means "Keep It Simple Stupid [or Silly]". If you are ever in any of our training sessions, you will hear us talk about the 'Rule of 3'. The 'Rule of 3' is quite simple in that you can construct a speech or presentation with no more than three points, angles, or ideas/thoughts.

Create a message around something that is concise and can be easily absorbed by your audience. Anything more than the three can create panic or potentially dilute your message. After all, Twitter doesn't allow more than 280 characters, formerly 140. By the way, anything close to 280 can make your readers feel like they have been presented a 'novel', so stay away from being tempted to use all your allowed characters. Fewer characters will force you to be creative in how you convey your message. This idea of less will be beneficial for your listeners and it will help to make your ideas and message vivid and clear within your own mind.

[49]

Steps For Developing An Outline

1. ***Opening remarks or statements***. This often is where your introduction comes. This is where you can establish yourself as an authority or subject matter expert on the topic you are presenting. Start with a bang - a strong opening. You can include a strong fact, statement, statistic, or even a story.
2. ***Premise***. This is the big idea that you are selling them and the reason for your presentation.
3. ***Body of the message***. As we shared earlier, consider using the Rule of 3, which will support your objective. The 'Rule of 3' is the key points or the key elements of your topic or subject.
4. ***Call to action or CTA***. *What do you want the audience to know or do?*
5. ***Close***. The conclusion is where you summarize your material. The close should tie back to the opening. This is where you can insert the overall lesson or idea that the audience should walk away with. This is where you can provide a final motivational or inspirational thought. Much like your opening, your close should also be powerful and memorable. You can tie back to an earlier story or point, use a fact, or even leave a charge.

Speech Outline With A Presentation Mind Map Approach

There are several creative ways for taking ideas and narrowing them down for your speech. This brainstorming method begins simply with your objective being placed in the middle of a page. After you write your objective, you then draw a larger circle around it. Then you draw out two to three circles that serve as the points or meat of your message. Should you consider a presentation mind map as the brainstorming tool of choice, then know that you can also use a whiteboard or open an app/document designed for this. This is a simple map for collecting ideas of what will be included in the speech. Remember that this and the other methods for developing your message should reflect that acronym KISS or keep it simple silly as you will likely be challenged with a multitude of ideas and not know where to begin. This will help you to organize and prioritize your thoughts.

1. ***Ask*** yourself if you can say what your speech is in a single sentence? If you cannot, then it may either be too complicated or confusing. It must be clear.
2. ***Write down*** what the headline or objective is in the center or top half of the page/whiteboard. Everything begins here and then branches or extends outward.
3. ***Remember*** and use the 'Rule of 3'. The three supporting points that reinforce your headline or overall objective. Write these connected with a line back to the headline or main objective of the speech. Feel free to also break these out onto separate sheets of paper/separate sections of the

whiteboard if additional room is needed. As stated earlier, anything more can overwhelm or complicate the message.

4. *Elaborate* upon the three points even further and reinforce them with examples, statistics, or even stories. This is the supportive material and the data to back up your point. This will allow for creativity and solidify not only your objective but provide credibility for you as the subject matter expert or as one who has the authority to speak on that subject. Consider your audience when using statistics or injecting terminology or acronyms. You may also require more room, so implement a system of color-coding or symbols to stay organized within this portion of supportive material.

5. *Feel free* to let loose with pictures and or symbols to help align your ideas.

6. *List* possible powerful openings and unforgettable closings.

Speech Outline With A Diamond Approach

Another model to consider is the diamond. This is where you picture the shape of the diamond with the top becoming your beginning. The middle is where you develop your presentation and then the bottom of the diamond or where the message comes to an end. An example of this can be your stated objective as the top of the diamond. What is in it for your hearers? Then you get into the meat of your message with no more than two to three things or points. The end is where you summarize the 3 points and bring the conclusion as stated in your opening objective. Here is where many will place a call to action or a takeaway.

Speech Outline With A Linear Approach

Older but for some a trusted linear approach or the methodology of using Roman Numerals and alphabet letters. For example, you would begin with Roman Numeral I and then underneath that have A, B & C. You would then proceed to Roman Numeral II and III with both being like the first with A, B & C. This approach could prove a challenge as you try to organize your thoughts and ideas before you develop them. Others taking this approach may also use notecards. This can be very helpful if you know what you are doing or if you are coached in the process.

Message Development
Prepare, Prepare, Prepare

Ask: Why you? What is the problem you are trying to solve? What are you trying to highlight? This is when you ask what your goal is? Who is your audience? Now is the time to brainstorm, now is the time to try the presentation mind map. Dedicate the appropriate time to brainstorm. This can be a great exercise to define and refine your message. What is your objective? What is

[51]

your 'why'? What is your reason? This needs to be on the forefront before you begin to lay out an outline of your presentation. Do you want to inform (educate) or motivate your audience?

Ultimately, you are looking to influence and shape the minds of your audience. You want them to feel something, do something, or think in a certain kind of way. Plan to stick within your allotted time. If you are asked to present for 45 minutes, then you may want to time your speech for 40 minutes. It is rude to run over your time and may lead to you not receiving an invitation back to speak again.

Organize & Outline
Organize & outline your speaking points as described earlier in this chapter. Pending the occasion and time allotted, you will know the number of bullet points to use. The message needs to make sense to the audience. You need to be relatable and know how much time to spend on 'setting the scene' and when to jump into your message. You may not want to spend too much time laying out information that they may already know. Why is this important to note: because you can love your data to the point of overload instead of looking at the data to support the message itself. Don't fall so in love with your data that your audience gets overwhelmed and lost trying to keep up.

Once you have established the end goal - the place you want to take the audience and leave the audience - it will be easier to put together the message itself. When crafting your message, it is important to look at a system that will work for you. It is important to have structure - one that can be repeatable and easy to follow. Compiling your thoughts word for word may not initially produce that desired outline. You should look for flexibility and a greater opportunity for your personality, expertise, and experience to come through. Here are several ways you can organize your thoughts.

Find Your Voice (Style, Creativity - Authentic Self)
Instead of creating a false speaker persona based on who you think others want you to be, we want you to discover your natural voice and then speak with power and authenticity. This will help you not come across as boring or what is known as the imposter syndrome. According to the Harvard Review, imposter syndrome can be defined as a collection of feelings or a belief system of inadequacy that can persist despite evident success. This is pretending to be something that you are not because of self-doubt. Signs of imposter syndrome include anxiety, feelings of inadequacy, doubting your abilities, dwelling on past mistakes, and comparing yourself to a different person or image.

When you speak with your voice, you will be able to convey the message with more clarity, passion, and sincerity. Without this, you can come across as fake, insincere, or stiff. When you are creating your presentation, we want to hear you - the essence of who you are. I want your message to resonate and your

Talk It Up! - A Guide To Successful Public Speaking

heart to be felt by all who are there. Don't be an actor but find your voice and speak. When you discover what your true voice or speaking style is, then study other speakers and speeches that reflect that style. As far as speaking voices or styles go, here are a few to consider:

Practice, Practice, Practice
We encourage you to watch the TEDx our friend and fellow speaker Gerald Leonard delivered entitled, 'What if Practice is the Performance?[2]' You can find the link to this talk in the endnotes and additional resources section of this book.

Read your presentation aloud and ask if it sounds natural. Record yourself giving the presentation. Ask a trusted friend, colleague, or family member to listen and provide feedback. Practice until it comes across as being natural and a reflection of your true voice. This will allow you to focus more on the audience and feed off them while you are feeding them.

Important Notes About Openings & Closings
According to Forbes[3], within the first seven seconds of meeting you, people will have a solid impression of who you are. Interesting is that research also suggests that it takes about a tenth of a second to start determining traits like trustworthiness. You have seven seconds, so make them count. This is an area we at DSB Leadership Group help our partners and clients to identify and focus on. How are they coming across to their clients and target market? This is a clear window of opportunity that should not be taken lightly. It is very difficult to bring the audience back if you messed this up.

If you are on a program or if you are being introduced, avoid introducing yourself again. This will eat into your speech and potentially distract them or take them away from truly hearing your message. The opening needs to grab their attention. It tells them to stop what they are thinking about and to focus on you. It piques curiosity, lets them know you have the authority to speak, and builds rapport.

Never, never start with an apology. Don't begin by stating something about you being nervous or about how difficult it was to put your presentation together. Do not paint a negative image in their minds when there is so much positivity and potential inspiration that will come because of you being there.

What have you got to lose? Start with a bang. Take a risk. You can use a quotation, visualization/illustration, statistics, a story, or a fact(s). Begin with a statement that will grab the audience's attention. Think about the news when you hear or see the words "breaking news". Then something is thrown right at you. Something that is meant to grab your attention. Your job is to grab their attention and pique their curiosity enough for them to pay attention. You can

[53]

Talk It Up! - A Guide To Successful Public Speaking

have attention grabbers not only in the beginning but also throughout your presentation. Other examples of ways to grab their attention include using an analogy, a quote, asking a question, stating some interesting fact, statistic, or even with a story (personal or an applicable one). This will not only get their attention, but it will also help your audience remember your message.

If you decide to use humor to kick off your presentation, please make sure you consider your audience and ensure it is tasteful or appropriate. Also please take note that should you use any quote, fact, or story about others, you have the proper citation. Give credit where credit is due. Stating the citation will also give credibility to your message.

When to use or when not to use certain illustrations, crude humor, or even profanity. We have seen too many speakers start to use profanity to build or arouse an audience when they have felt they were starting to lose them. We personally believe that is more reflective of the speaker than of the audience. Be mindful as gestures, words and even symbols can carry a different meaning depending on where you are.

Closing your speech. Make sure you stop before your audience stops listening. Make them feel and think a certain way. Consider summarizing and using a compelling call to action. Remember visualization or a story to tie back into the beginning and main point of your speech. Every point should be built upon the intro and heart of your message. Do not close your speech or presentation by saying 'it was great to be here'. What will leave the audience thinking 'now I need to do something with what I received'.

What will they do because of your presentation? How did it add value to their lives? How will it make them feel after they leave their time with you? How you should handle feedback as well as a time for Questions & Answers will be addressed later in this book. Note that this can be invaluable for strengthening your message or a potential danger to derailing your message and damaging your credibility.

Be respectful of your audience by being mindful of your time. When you are given an allotted time to present, do whatever it takes to stay within it. It is a 'cardinal sin' when speakers take the liberty to go on beyond the time given to them.

Remember that you began with a bang and now you must end with one as well. What do you want them to remember? What do you want them to do? Pick up your energy and consider your tempo. You can summarize and you can close with a story - one that is imprinted on their minds.

[54]

Talk It Up! - A Guide To Successful Public Speaking

Timing & Length

The length of your message will depend on several factors including your rate of speech and on the allotted time you are given. Keep your audience in mind as this may mean adjusting your rate of speech.

Here is a simple guide that we use and train on when given certain lengths of time to speak. If you are asked to speak within five minutes, then perhaps formulate your speech around a single point. If given 30 minutes, then consider up to three points.

Whatever you do, never go longer than the allotted time. It is better to end a little early than to feel as if you must rush through your presentation or be tempted to go beyond your allotted time. This also conveys to the audience that you are not prepared or 'polished' enough to stay disciplined with your delivery. If you are working with an event organizer, clarify the amount of time and if it is customary to include a Q&A or feedback period.

To Memorize Or Not To Memorize

We do not recommend memorizing your speech or presentation word for word. Doing this could lead to you sounding robotic and lacking authenticity. Instead, focus more on keywords or a phrase; something you build off and easily remember such as a story or acronym.

There are ways to help remember your presentation including the development of mini-stories and the practice of grounding. Mini-stories are just that: they are acronyms or very short stories that you create to aid your ability to move your overall message along. Each part of the mini-story or acronym represents a point, story, and transition for your overall message.

You can also mark areas of the stage to begin each section or point of your message. The beginning or opening would be in the center of the stage. You would then move to another spot to remind yourself to begin the next point. After stating that point, you can then move freely on the stage. This can continue for every point you have. Another image to consider is that of your home. Walk through the main door for the welcome, imagine what would be said as you walked into the living room, and then the kitchen.

Grounding is a way to both remind yourself that you are safe and can serve to identify when to move or transition within your presentation. Touching your pinky could signal the first point. Grabbing your ring finger could help transition you to make your next point and so on. You cannot make this so obvious that it becomes a distraction.

[55]

Talk It Up! - A Guide To Successful Public Speaking

Reflection
1. *How* do you form your presentations?
2. *What* have you found to work in creating a simple yet memorable presentation?

CHAPTER 7
Rehearse, Then Crush

Don't buy into the saying that practice makes perfect. That may sound inspiring, but it is not realistic. Instead, try looking at practice from this perspective: practice makes progress. Progress is a much better word for reinforcing positive behavior and strengthening your belief system. What we want to encourage and emphasize is that you must incorporate practice as a part of your strategy for a successful presentation. There is another saying that if you don't plan for success, then you are planning for failure.

We've found that most would equate the amount of work they put into writing their speech or the time they put into creating their presentation is enough or in some way will make up for the lack of rehearsing. They put more actual time into the creation than into the practice of delivering. This is not a formula for success. You must put in the time to say your speech out loud. You must practice speaking with your slides and visual aids. A live or real-time rehearsal is crucial for ensuring a successful outcome.

Your rehearsal should provide feedback on what you should keep, do or adjust before your presentation. You will become more comfortable with your content and ability to deliver with confidence. Rehearsing will help to keep you focused on your goal and not become deterred by distractions, the audience's reaction, or your own nerves. You will ultimately be assured of your content being spot on. Your notes, script, outline, and aids are there to support you and not the other way around. Practice will validate that.

Confidence Through Preparation
Every athlete and musician will tell you that they practice a shot, stroke, note, key, or piece of music repeatedly until it becomes second nature. This muscle memory comes from thousands of the same or repeated processes. This is the foundation of confidence.

A Right Way And A Wrong Way
Every coach will tell you that there is such a thing as a right way and a wrong way to prepare. The wrong approach is to go at it without a plan. There really is a 'method to the madness'. There is a specific plan focused on the area of need. We all are tempted to gravitate to the areas we are strong in and yet, it is those areas we deem not as strong that warrant the attention. So, ask yourself, do I have a plan for this area of my skill set? Do I have a plan to prepare for success?

Talk It Up! - A Guide To Successful Public Speaking

Practice as if in real-time. Practice with the same energy, focus, and passion as if you are in front of your live audience. Use the same body language you envision yourself using when you deliver the message. Use the same vocal variety and language as well. If possible, practice with the technology you will be using when delivering your speech. Here is a bonus: if possible, visit and practice in the space you will be eventually speaking in. Walk around the venue, know how big the stage is and if you can move about.

I (David) would be remiss if I did not personally share that as a minister who has officiated over 75 weddings, I remind the wedding party to never lock their knees. I have thankfully never had an incident but have witnessed weddings where members of the party have fainted or excuse the imagery here, have vomited because of the lack of proper blood flow from their knees being locked. Relax and slightly flex your legs.

There is such a charming and gratifying element to a smile. A perfectly timed smile can be disarming and equally inviting.

In your rehearsals, ensure that you practice not only your introduction and closing, but that you factor in your body language, including your movement around the stage if that is afforded to you. Every element, including how you 'enter the scene' or take to the stage matters and should be practiced. Sit, stand and move with anticipation. Don't be shy, go ahead and practice receiving that Academy Award. Think back to the power of visualization.

Being present is key and practicing with this mindset will help ensure a successful presentation.

It is also worth noting that you need to practice the correct form, key, pitch, etc. repeatedly. Practicing the wrong motion, key, and pitch will ultimately lead to discouragement as the result will not equal the desired intention.

Memorize It All Or Not

From our experience in coaching and training on speaking, we have discovered that most of our students and clients benefit more from preparing their message with cues or points and not from memorizing their entire presentation.

Unless you are an actor, we do not encourage our clients to memorize everything within their presentation word for word. Very few can do this, and your audience will be more impressed by your authenticity than your ability to memorize your presentation. This may be a waste of time and energy. Attempting to memorize every detail of your presentation can lead you to sound robotic, overly rehearsed, and not authentic.

[58]

Talk It Up! - A Guide To Successful Public Speaking

Robert wanted to make sure he did not leave anything out of his presentation. He wanted to deliver a perfect message and decided that it would be best to memorize every word, line by line. When he got up to speak, he drew a blank, and then anxiety took over. He wanted to impress the audience and his peers by speaking from memory and without notes, only to resort to his notes.

We worked with Rob on various techniques including memorizing bullet points or committing to memory a sequence or a story within a story. This is where you arrange ideas in a logical sequence based on time or space. For example, you can build the presentation around a story which has:

1. *Past*, present, and future
2. *Steps* as in 1, 2 & 3
3. *Rooms* in a home
4. *Spacing* on the stage

When using Past, Present, and Future, you would arrange your presentation in an order that would follow a story highlighting a prior event, a current situation, and a future outcome. You practice each portion of the story.

Using Steps '1, 2, and 3' is building your practice around something that logically makes sense in sequential order. First comes step 1 and then logically step 2 comes next, followed by step 3.

The latter two are visualization techniques where you use what you know to form your speech or presentation around. When you enter the house, you naturally will come into the great room and use your first point to in a way describe what is in that room. Your second point will naturally stem from recognizing elements from within the next room, say the kitchen.

The spacing technique is about building within your memory where you'll be standing as you share your first point. And when you move to the next place on the stage, there your second point begins, etc.

Regarding the bullet points, you can even have the bullet points begin with a keyword or have them complete an acronym, which can be helpful for moving a message along.

What Else Could You Try?
We might suggest that you not only rehearse on your own but that you consider inviting others to listen to you rehearse. Invite family, trusted friends, and peers to listen in and provide feedback.

[59]

Talk It Up! - A Guide To Successful Public Speaking

Please set expectations and provide direction before opening the floor for their thoughts. If you do not make clear what you need from them, you may end up regretting that you asked them to listen. Keep in mind that while well-intentioned, they may not have the experience as a speaking coach or as a speaker to constructively provide helpful feedback.

Let them know how much time you have been given, your topic, and what they should be listening for. You can even provide a 'checklist' or 'speaker review list' before you begin. This list can include time, vocal variety use, use of body language, storytelling and imagery, technology use, and overall impact - if the objective was met. Ask for no more than one or two areas to improve so as to not become overwhelmed with feelings of failure or disappointment. Inversely they can share or state all the good things or elements of your presentation.

We also suggest that you record yourself rehearsing. This is important as you know better than anyone else what your intentions are and how you hope your message will be received.

James asked if we could sit and listen to him deliver a presentation before his actual presentation. This was an incredible opportunity to learn what areas of his presentation were on point and which areas if any would need to be addressed. With his allotted time and technology in mind, we watched with anticipation and were happy to provide constructive input. This practice without interruption provided incredible insight and 'set the stage' for him to crush his actual presentation. We are happy to say that he indeed delivered. Way to go, James!

Remember - Mindset & Control
Think back to Chapter 6 when we touch on the 'Rule of 3'. Points must be simple or brief, specific, and actionable. This is what will help your points become memorable.

One thing that makes our company DSB Leadership Group different from many other communications and training organizations is that we add mindset modules or workshops. We believe strongly that you can have all the resources and yet fail to deliver/achieve your speaking goals if you are not first convinced in your own mind that you are more than capable/more than adequate to deliver a successful message.

Get that BS out of your mind. You and I may not be thinking the same. I want you to get rid of that Bad Script and change that Belief System. That's not going to be helpful for you, that's just baloney. You are incredible so practice from that view.

As a part of our coaching philosophy, we ask our clients often about which elements are in their control versus those factors that are out of their control.

[60]

Talk It Up! - A Guide To Successful Public Speaking

We then channel their focus on those within their control. They can control their mindset and attitude; as well as their preparation, which includes contingencies such as technology failing or the weather not cooperating. They also cannot control the audience's response or attitude, scheduling changes, or venue or room temperature mishaps. Don't allow yourself to be consumed or overtaken by what you cannot control.

Practice All The Time

Take every opportunity to practice, practice and practice. Try to present whenever and wherever possible. Look for opportunities within weekly meetings, reviews, sales presentations, Church or Religious functions, PTAs, associations, and community events.

The more you rehearse the less dependent you will become on your notes and slides. Remember that practice makes progress and the more your confidence will grow. This practice will produce that incredible outcome of an excellently delivered presentation.

Stay authentic and remember you are most likely to advance the runner if you stay within the comfort of your own batting stance. In other words, be yourself and don't try to be somebody else. Finding your own 'batting stance' is an illustration from baseball we often share in our training. Not all the players enter the batter's box with the same stance. They enter with a stance that they are most comfortable with. For those of us that love the sport, we may struggle with the length of the game and all of the rituals and habits that these incredible athletes go through; but we appreciate that whatever their stance, it works for them, and we need them to be comfortable and confident to be at their best and to perform to the level of expecting a win.

Activity
- *Write* in a journal about your experiences during your own rehearsals.

CHAPTER 8
Master Fillers & Vocal Variety

We can all likely recall a conversation or presentation that was lost in 'translation' because the discussion was peppered with filler words.

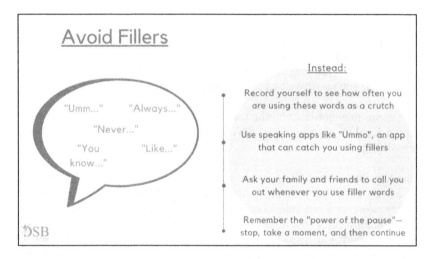

What are filler words and why might you want to be aware of them? Filler words are nothing more than short words or phrases used when speaking to 'fill' in the gaps between thoughts, sentences, and topics. They are often used during moments of silence, hesitation, and if we are being gracious even in times of uncertainty. This can be a result of a lack of awareness, lack of practice, or even insecurity. Silence can be just as uncomfortable as uncertainty is when not knowing what to say next.

Some of the more common filler words might include 'um', 'er', 'like', 'oh', 'okay', 'you know', 'basically', 'and', 'to be honest', 'actually', 'just', 'I mean', 'so', 'well', and 'uh'. Overuse of these can make the presenter seem unprepared and uncertain and drown out the audience as they can become very distracting. We don't want you to think that you will become robotic in trying to make perfect statements or speeches. We know that a filler from time to time may make you sound relatable. We want to be aware of them, your potential usage of them, and eventually, you to have a mastery over your speech.

Don't play the Umm Game. Umms and uhhs cannot become placeholders for what's next. They can become what the audience hears instead of your message.

Most know that they use them. Most even know why they tend to use them. We are asked often about how to remove or get rid of these words and their reliance upon them. The logical progression of our students is a growing awareness and reduction in reliance upon these filler words.

Where Do Fillers Occur?
Fillers typically begin at the beginning of a statement, sentence, thought, or topic. Consider how often you hear one when someone is responding to a question or when they are transitioning to a new topic.

Here is an example of something you might hear from a press conference, following a basketball game:
"Coach, was the last play of the game executed the way you drew it up?"
"Um, well, you know we had to script the perfect play."

The coach may not have felt he was being defensive, but the response begins with a level of uncertainty - a level of not knowing what to initially say in responding.

Another time fillers will appear is when there are moments of 'dead space' or when you have lost yourself (your words, your thoughts, your place in your presentation, or even your confidence). Silence can be dangerous as it is a common moment where insecurity can lead to the addition of fillers. We want you to be okay with silence. Silence can be your ally. Remember that you are in control. Use that silence to find your place, capture your thoughts, and allow your audience a moment to digest, and prepare for your next words.

When you make a point or provide an illustration, you will want to allow a moment for the audience and their brains to decide how to store and use what was said. If you make a point and leave no pause and immediately deliver another point, then the first point has been minimized, neutralized, or rendered unimportant. They could inevitably forget aspects of the first point entirely. Use the power of the pause and the audience will digest your point and store it in a way that is memorable. At the end of the day, how did you make them feel? Frustrated by all the 'noise' or enlightened and inspired by your message?

The other place where you might hear filler words from a speaker or presenter is during moments of transition. It is perfectly fine to say, 'point number 2' or you can just go into your next point. This transition does not need to be awkward.

Talk It Up! - A Guide To Successful Public Speaking

Practice

As you gain more experience as a speaker, you will become more aware of the dangers of using fillers like 'umm', 'uh' and 'you know'. You may also work on avoiding or at least limiting words such as always and never. These can be distracting and draw the audience to listen to why you said 'always' and 'never' and take away from your message.

How do you minimize these fillers? Mindfulness and practice. Mindfulness takes discipline. Mindfulness takes into consideration your audience. Also, practice makes it better.

Try recording yourself speaking and go back to see how often you are using this as a crutch. I've heard some of my competitors or other professionals within my space tell their clients to not record themselves to avoid becoming overly critical of themselves. It is exceedingly difficult to improve upon your ability to deliver incredible presentations without taking the time to hear yourself speak. When you know yourself and your tendencies and you can adjust, you will become that much more of an effective speaker.

You can also ask friends to listen to your speeches or practice using a speaking app like Ummo - an app that serves to support your growth and catch you when you use those fillers. If you are not aware of them, you will continue to use them.

Invest in your growth with courses, resources, and the use of a speaking coach (DSB Leadership Group). We work with our clients and students to capture and master this aspect of public speaking.

Confidence

Confidence goes a long way in supporting a speaker's ability to manage their filler words. Our clients continue to share how the 'Mindset Workshops' have helped their leaders grow in grasping the concepts and training around public speaking. Most athletes and performers will also tell you that what separates the very best is not talent, but the mind. There is an air of confidence that the very elite have. Your confidence in being able to manage your own expectations, breathing, and message will lead to incredible impact. Remember that speaking is about influence and that starts with influencing yourself.

Mindset tip: become comfortable with silence. This is extremely important. Silence for many speakers can seem to indicate that something is wrong, and the temptation will be to continue even without pausing or to add fillers. Don't fill in the silence with fillers. Embrace silence. As we mentioned earlier, silence

[65]

Talk It Up! - A Guide To Successful Public Speaking

can be to your advantage as it can provide a moment to let what was just said permeate. Let them reflect on your message before moving to the next point.

Discover and experiment with creative ways of communicating and expressing your message.

The Power of the Pause

You will find throughout this book and whenever you come across our training, the frequency of our mention of the 'power of the pause'. There are a few phrases you will likely hear repeatedly if you are in our training, workshops, or a part of our Social Media Groups. One of those is "The Power of the Pause". There is incredible power in being able to use well-timed pauses. Being silent accomplishes a few things: Gives you a moment to gather your thoughts, manipulate the crowd, give them time to digest what you just said, and help you control the proverbial "umm". Practice pausing and learn when to use them. These go a long way to helping speakers avoid those filler words as pausing can convey intelligence and deep thought. So, take a deep breath and collect your thoughts.

Pausing allows you that split moment to collect your thoughts and regain control of your message. Pausing can also help your message by creating excitement and suspense. The audience cannot wait to receive what is going to come out of your mouth. As mentioned already, pauses will allow the audience a much-needed moment to soak in what you've just shared.

Master Cadence & Vocal Variety

There has been plenty of research into the importance of cadence and vocal variety.

What does the cadence of your speech mean? Is there such a thing as speaking too fast? Speed, tempo, and rhythm are vital when used appropriately. Changing the pace or rhythm will affect how an audience will experience a presentation or speech. When a speaker strategically changes the cadence, the message can be received more easily and can take the most challenging or 'boring' content and make it seem interesting.

There are people that tend to speak quickly when they are nervous or when they are very excited as adrenaline can be pumping through their body. If you know that this is you, you can actually plan for this very early in your preparation process. You can learn how to master your cadence in your speech. Do everything you can through practice, preparation, and affirmation in awareness to master your opportunity.

Talk It Up! - A Guide To Successful Public Speaking

Do not confuse energy and excitement with a great speech. While those are essential, they can be misleading if they are there due to a lack of control. This is not a contest to determine who can say the most in the least amount of time. The speed and pace of your speech can reflect not knowing the power of your position and it can become in a way a filler. Focus more on comprehension and you will gain more control of your speed.

You will also want to limit the amount of caffeine and anything else that could speed up your adrenaline. Also, ensure a proper amount of rest and sleep and that you put in the time to prepare before you deliver that presentation.

Vocal Variety
Any speaker that is monotone will come across as boring and boring equates to low impact and low influence. Heaven forbid that a keynote speaker presents in the same volume, tone, and cadence throughout their entire message. Recall the example from the Clear Eyes commercials with Ben Stein[1] and how his tagline is simple 'wow'. He doesn't change his tone or cadence and yet, it works for the brand. While that may work for a 15-second commercial, it will not likely work for a 20 or 40-minute presentation.

Be creative and consider the impact you want to have throughout your presentation. Consider your pitch, cadence, and tone. Mix it up and discover the impact that can be made with these elements.

A note on allotted time: We want to encourage you not to get caught up with the feeling that you could be inconveniencing your audience by taking the entire allotted time given to you. The best thing you could do is give the audience your full attention and deliver the information in a way that can best be received. Give your audience time to digest or soak in your point before transitioning or moving forward in your presentation. Consider that commas, periods, and exclamation points are there for a reason. When you give your presentation, keep that in mind and it will help you to slow down.

Activity
1. ***Read*** a paragraph out loud from your favorite book or even this book. Say that paragraph again but add a few pauses. Notice the difference when you creatively and strategically add pauses.
2. ***Next***, enlist a friend or peer and ask them to present you with a topic. Ask them to set a 2-minute time limit and then to listen for fillers. The more you practice, the more you will see yourself being in control of the moment and thoughts.

[67]

CHAPTER 9
Storytelling

You may have heard of the following saying, 'facts tell, but stories sell'. While this may not be your strength or voice, a well-timed story can be a powerful tool to engage your audience. A well-timed story can change everything. A story has the power of being able to paint a picture in the minds of your audience. Stories can invoke incredible feelings and stir not only the emotions of the audience but captivate their imaginations.

Steve Jobs once stated, "the most powerful person in the world is the storyteller. The storyteller sets the vision, values, and agenda of an entire generation that is to come."[1] Do you believe that you can become a great storyteller? Let's look into what you should know about storytelling.

There is a true tragedy in not telling your story or in not using stories to support your message. Imagine all the stories that have not been told- that have not been heard. My (David) family had an idea that was born from serving Assisting living and Retirement communities. We would serve our treasures by reading to them, playing games with them, and even (my daughter) would paint their nails. They gave more to us than we could ever give to them. They shared their stories and held nothing back as far as imagery goes.

This idea was given more life because of the health pandemic. The idea would be to partner with other writers and professionals to create an archive of interviews. This project of writing mini memoirs to capture these stories is not just for those residents, but also for their families. We are not far from launching this and could use some of you who are reading this to get involved.

When it comes to stories, what should you know? Specify details. The Five W formula: who, what, when, where, and why. This gives life and details.

Tip: Be so dramatic! This is the opposite of what we did not want to see in our children unless they wanted a career in acting. Use your body language and strong dialogue delivery.

Relatable & Personable
It certainly can be personal - reflect on your own life - own experiences. This level of transparency is vital to the success of the speech. There is an incredible

Talk It Up! - A Guide To Successful Public Speaking

opportunity to connect by sharing from your life what we would phrase as authentically modest personal narratives. We can all pull up instances from our youth and professional life that will connect with our audience.

The key is asking how you want the audience to feel and not just think. This is the power of stories. People will listen if the story captivates them. They listen because they want to hear how the story ends. Where you want the audience to get to is how you choose or place the right story. Start with that end goal in mind. This helps the audience follow or grasp progress-they are moved along by the story.

Most stories contain some form of conflict or hardship within them. There are ups and downs. This conveys relatability. Does the hero save the day? Do the guy and girl get together? Does the main character win in the end?

Start the story by painting a picture. This is where you set the scene. The start can be as simple as the words 'Imagine if''. Use vibrant, colorful language. The story should cause the audience to feel involved and even react to what is being shared. Make the story evoke emotion. Yes, don't be afraid to go there and make it emotional. Make them laugh, cry or fill them with a sense of wonder and conviction. Tell the story and show the story. Use your expressions and body language to show the story. How does the story end? What is the moral of the story? This is the takeaway.

Keep in mind that a story needs to be relatively short in nature. Do not make the stories too long or people will feel as if you cannot deliver a punchline or prove what the moral of the story is. My attention goes from being captivated to being distracted like a goldfish or the canine from the Disney & Pixar movie *Up*[2].

What are some of your favorite stories? Why those? What impact have they had in your life?

There is a great video on storytelling by David JP Phillips, entitled 'The Magical Science of Storytelling'[3]. You can find the link to this talk in the endnotes and additional resources section of this book.

Activity
Tell a story about the current weather that will move others emotionally. Illustration: Crisp cool morning. Leaves scratching the ground while being guided by the brisk wind. Smells of a smoldering fireplace.
1. *Make* it memorable
2. *Make* it relatable
3. *It does not need* to be funny, but it should evoke emotion

Talk It Up! - A Guide To Successful Public Speaking

Developing A Story - The Art Of Storytelling
By now you can see how stories can affect the way we feel and think. Stories can inspire you toward action or move you to tears. A great story will take an audience on a journey, igniting imagination and passion. Storytelling can start movements and end wars.

The best speakers often use stories as a powerful tool for demonstrating and bringing to life a key message. It's one of the best ways to make both your presentation and brand memorable. A juicy story will keep the audience on the edge of their seats - quite literally. A well-timed story can not only be impactful and accomplish the presenters' goal; a well-timed story can last in the mind of the audience for years.

Stories can also be a powerful tool in supporting businesses and leaders as they engage with their teams, departments, and clients/prospects. There is the added option of outsourcing and bringing in publicists and Public Relations firms.

Structuring your speech to get your ideas across and keeping your audience engaged can be tricky but it can be so effective when deployed at the right moment. What you will discover about storytelling is that it is truly an art form. Learn this art form and you will be painting incredible results in the minds of your audience.

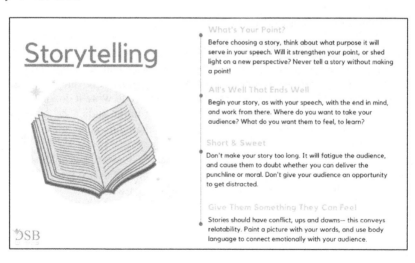

What's Your Point?
Before choosing a story, think about what purpose it will serve in your speech. Will it strengthen your point, or shed light on a new perspective? Never tell a story without making a point!

All's Well That Ends Well
Begin your story, as with your speech, with the end in mind, and work from there. Where do you want to take your audience? What do you want them to feel, to learn?

Short & Sweet
Don't make your story too long. It will fatigue the audience, and cause them to doubt whether you can deliver the punchline or moral. Don't give your audience an opportunity to get distracted.

Give Them Something They Can Feel
Stories should have conflict, ups and downs— this conveys relatability. Paint a picture with your words, and use body language to connect emotionally with your audience.

Talk It Up! - A Guide To Successful Public Speaking

When incorporating storytelling in your public speaking or presentations, keep the following in mind:

1. **Begin** with the end in mind. How will the story tie back into your presentation or speech's overall objective?
2. **Tell** a personal story or make it personal and never be afraid of being vulnerable. This will help to create relatability. Few things are as captivating as a personal story, especially those of triumph over extreme adversity.
3. **Keep** it truthful. If it is not a fact, then clearly state that before or after you share the story.
4. **What** do you want your audience to feel? Immerse the audience in your story by providing sensory details and colorful language. Details that will allow them to in a way see, hear, feel, and smell the different stimuli in your story world.
5. **Craft** the story by setting the scene. This provides context to which the story comes into play within the overall scheme of your presentation or speech.
6. **Create** suspense. Those who love to watch movies or read books know that a good story always has to have a conflict and a plot. These two elements are what make a good presentation become a roller coaster ride that is thrilling with both highs and lows. The audience will throughout the story ask themselves, "What will happen next?"
7. **Be** willing to use the entire spectrum of emotion and match the tone and body language.
8. **End** with something memorial

Tip: If you don't have a journal, get one. You can use various journals to capture your own thoughts (reflect), capture your victories and accomplishments (victory journal), and even for stories that you hear or even develop, that can be used to support your future presentations. You have to write it down - get it out of your mind and think about how it can impact future audiences. You can even use your phone/voice recorders and separate them into categories.

Make the complex simple. We do not all need to know what studies and understanding go into the mechanics of an engine, some of us just want to know when we put the key in or press that button that the car will start.

Activity
1. **Tell** your story - there is only one you! Facts tell but stories sell.
2. **What** are some stories that every professional and business needs to tell?

[72]

CHAPTER 10
To Tech Or Not To Tech

Likely, you've heard of the saying that something can be both 'a blessing and a curse'. This is when something is either both a benefit and a burden or when something may seem initially beneficial but also brings unforeseen negative consequences. While technology can greatly enhance the listening experience; technology could be that blessing or that curse for every speaker or presenter. At one moment tech can aid greatly in your presentation and in a split second, it can backfire. When not used properly, however, technology can become a barrier to effective listening.

What would you do if the tech supporting you and your presentation collapsed? Because technology can fail you, you should always be prepared to go on without the technology. This reminds us of another saying, that you should 'hope for the best but prepare for the worst'. What's your backup plan? This more than implies that you should always have a backup plan. Back up that file, print off that presentation and send your presentation beforehand to the program organizer or event planner.

Technology is brilliant and should work for you instead of you working for technology. You need to have a full grasp of the technology that you are using. In other words, if you are not familiar with the technology, then don't use that stage or time of your presentation for integrating the tech. Work out the kinks on your own.

Technology should never be the primary factor when planning for a successful presentation. If you rely on technology too much and something goes wrong, you're in trouble. Technology is brilliant but it should be something that follows you, rather than you following it.

What Should You Know About Technology?
In presentations, do make the best use of technology but do not overuse it. Always remember that the goal is communicating with and guiding the minds of your audience. As mentioned earlier, technology can enhance your presentation, but it cannot become your presentation. Should you implement or integrate technology?

Technology Tools

Some technology tools that can be useful include:

- *Wireless clicker* to advance slides from wherever you are
- *Laser pointer:* beware of over-using this and avoid pointing at your audience with this tool
- *Stage microphones and speakers* to ensure the audience can hear
- *Roving microphones*, so everyone can hear what questions the audience asks
- *Autocues* (for politicians who do not have time to read carefully prepared speeches)
- *Stage and audience lighting*
- *Music:* including background music and music/videos to be used during your presentation.
- *Live connection to the internet* for real-time and real-world information.
- *Side screens/side monitors* containing relevant information or a live stream of the presentation, showing audience interactions and comments.

Technology Tips

Here are a few things to keep in mind when considering technology or illustrations:

1. Do A Check

Check with the venue and the event or program coordinator to confirm the technology including any props can indeed be used and that your presentation format is compatible with their technology. This may require you to send over your material before the event or to even show up and conduct a dry run. You may not want to use a technology you are not as familiar with. We have been there, and it can be embarrassing.

The speaker should always do a test run to make sure that everything is set up properly to avoid malfunction or hiccups later during the speech. If possible, the speaker should also do a soundcheck. Amplified or not, at the beginning of the speech, the speaker should not have to ask, "Can you hear me in the back?"

What is your backup should something go wrong? Always be prepared as this can and does happen. Can you go and crush it without relying on slides and videos?

2. Integrate

Consider the technology they are asking you to work with. Can you integrate the technology with your presentation? This goes without saying, but you need to factor in the state of the technology and if it is current, updated, and able to 'work' with. Will they present you with a microphone? If they present you with one, do not turn it down. They know their venue better than you do and it may not be appropriate to tell the audience that you are loud enough for them to hear you. Is it a handheld? Is it wireless? Also, please always assume that the mic is on because it may be.

3. Bring Your Own Device (BYOD)
Bringing your own device is a way of saying that you can trust what has been in your control and that is your own tech. If it works on your laptop, then try to use your own laptop. Don't forget to turn the screensaver off on your computer. Make sure the computer doesn't go into sleep mode. Turn off any notifications and applications such as MSN Messenger. If you've set up your email on Outlook, beware of a little banner that pops up at the bottom of the screen alerting you to a new email.

4. Mind Your Manners
Before the presentation, the speaker should silence his or her cell phone or any other device that might make noise and provide an interruption. The audience should do the same. The speaker has the right to request that the audience complies with his or her desire to have a distraction-free environment. If you are working with an event organizer or planner, they likely would ask for audience support in this area.

Language and images should be considered before you regret not censoring yourself. Would the images or language you use be deemed offensive or inappropriate? Consider the culture and demographics of your audience as this may shape not only the usage of words and images (pictures) but the use of colors as well.

You can use almost anything as a prop but please make sure the prop is appropriate for the audience and to your boundaries as a speaker. Ensure that

Talk It Up! - A Guide To Successful Public Speaking

fonts are clear and large enough to be read. Do not overwhelm the eyes of your audience with too many images on one slide or prop. Simple and clean never goes out of style while loud and busy can seem overwhelming. Consider your audience but also factor in how your slides, or videos can take the audience away from you. We consult our clients before every presentation to ensure their presentations are both clean and clear. They should be simple and not take the attention away from the presenter. They are there to support, enhance and highlight.

Additional Tech Tools

Speaking of tech tools, there are a whole slew of them out there that go hand in hand with giving a first-class presentation. Check out the following apps to help take your public speaking skills to the next level:

- *Ummo*. This incredible app measures how often your students use filler words during a speech, such as "like", "um" and "you know". (Teachers - try using this when you're delivering a lesson and you may be surprised at the results!)
- *Metronome app*. This type of app is perfect for helping your students pace themselves. It measures their speaking rate, so they can tell when they've sped up because of nervousness. Some examples include Pro Metronome or Metronome Beats.
- *Mentimeter*. Technology makes your presentation more engaging and now, you can incorporate more interaction with your audience and find out what they have in mind. You can draw, edit, and add content to your presentation through technology.
- *PowerPoint3D*. Embedding a 3D model into your presentation can invite more interaction. This software can be used to highlight a product or a message by integrating rotation and zoom functions for better viewing.
- *Teleprompter app*. Remember that moment when you were in school, and you dropped your notecards? Make sure that never happens to you by downloading a teleprompter app, like the PromptSmart Lite Teleprompter. It's a fun way to help your students and make them feel like real news anchors!
- *Timer app*. Timing is everything in public speaking! Teach your students to keep track of their speaking time by using a timer app. The Toastmaster Timer app is a great one because it allows students to set the minimum and maximum time limits. Once the minimum time limit has passed, the screen turns green, as it nears the maximum time limit it's yellow, and if they've gone overtime it turns red.
- *VoiceVibes*[1]. Listen to episode 31 of our Twins Talk it Up podcast where we discuss with Debra Cancro the use of technology to help professionals become more effective speakers and presenters.[2] Mention DSB Leadership Group, and you may have an opportunity for a discounted plan.

- ***Virtual platforms*** such as Zoom, Microsoft Teams, and Skype. These virtual platforms allow for live-stream presentations. These allow audiences to join from 'remote' locations.
- ***Virtual Reality.*** VR is not for gaming alone. Technology advancements (and budget pending) now allow for greater creativity with audiences that are both able to plug in locally or remotely.

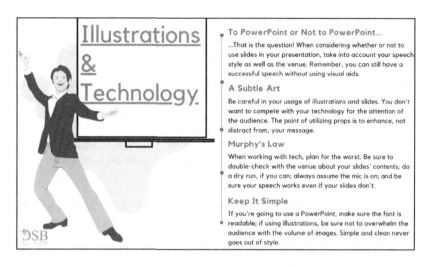

To PowerPoint or Not to PowerPoint...
...That is the question! When considering whether or not to use slides in your presentation, take into account your speech style as well as the venue. Remember, you can still have a successful speech without using visual aids.

A Subtle Art
Be careful in your usage of illustrations and slides. You don't want to compete with your technology for the attention of the audience. The point of utilizing props is to enhance, not distract from, your message.

Murphy's Law
When working with tech, plan for the worst. Be sure to double-check with the venue about your slides' contents; do a dry run, if you can; always assume the mic is on; and be sure your speech works even if your slides don't.

Keep It Simple
If you're going to use a PowerPoint, make sure the font is readable; if using illustrations, be sure not to overwhelm the audience with the volume of images. Simple and clean never goes out of style.

PowerPoint, Google Slides, & Slide Tips

To use or not to use slides, videos, props, or handouts? That is the question. There are varied opinions about this and so we will share with you ours. In the years of working with many professionals, we know that there can be an added factor, benefit, and dimension with slides and PowerPoints presentations. We love visual effects - visual aspects of any presentation. But before you give your next presentation and begin to create your PowerPoint or slide presentation, here are some things to keep in mind for crushing that next event.

At the top of the list should be your own style or 'batting stance'. Keep in mind the venue where you will be presenting. As we've alluded to earlier, you do not want to be competing with technology for the attention of the audience. Remember that technology should be viewed as a support to your presentation and not be the presentation itself. Remember that the goal is to connect and speak on a personal level. You need to know what would work best for you and your speaking style.

You should know your slides inside out. Remember that you must practice, practice and practice to ensure that you are properly prepared.

Ask, where do you want their focus to be? If that focus is to be on you, then do not put everything you are going to say on the slide or handout. Don't

Talk It Up! - A Guide To Successful Public Speaking

overwhelm your audience with too much information and too much clutter on the actual slide. Remember when preparing slides that less is indeed more. They are there to capture your audience's attention and move them along your journey. When properly placed and used, they can help your audience transition to the next point or further emphasize something you are speaking about. So, keep the slides clean with simple messages and not the entire message or presentation itself. Sometimes a picture can indeed be worth a thousand words so use them at the right time.

A good rule of thumb is to limit your slides to no more than three to five lines and to consider your font size. Typically, you want them larger than you may initially anticipate. Font size should be 24-point or larger. A tip would be to print out a few if not all your slides on standard paper and then place them on the floor. The slides are probably readable for your audience if you can read them while standing and looking down on them.

Use easy-to-read fonts such as Arial, Calibri, or Times New Roman. Avoid 'odd' fonts and graphics, when possible, unless it is your logo or within your logo

Keep in mind the effectiveness of using highlighters as the intention is to highlight something important. Slides are to highlight and not to become the entire presentation.

In your slides, if you are doing any type of 'before and after' or even a 'compare and contrast', consider the culture of the audience you are presenting to. Here in the Western Culture of the United States, we read from left to right and so it would be advisable to consider using the left side of your screen/slide to reflect your 'before' or 'compare' and the right side of your screen/slide for your 'after' or 'contrast'. You don't want to make your audience work to understand or try to figure out your intention with the images and wording you use. Keep it simple, work with your audience, and then they will work with you.

If you are feeling stuck and uncertain about slide design, there are plenty of templates out there for you, and a simple 'click, copy and paste' can bring your presentation to life.

We'd like to add this point: don't read directly from them and do not put your entire presentation on the screen (within the slide). Remember, that they are only there to support you and reinforce what you want to say, and the points you're trying to convey. Do not use your slides as a crutch. As was stated earlier, the slides are only there to aid you and compliment your message and presentation and not the other way around.

[78]

Talk It Up! - A Guide To Successful Public Speaking

Videos & Visual Aides

Along with our other senses, sight can play a vital role in learning. Should you incorporate videos within your presentation, be mindful of your audience, and time to ensure the video 'fits' with your presentation. The use of video itself creates or can aid a presentation by dramatically capturing the audience's attention and breaking up or providing a much-needed additive to the text and content of a potentially boring, bullet-point slide presentation. They cannot take away from nor present in the minds of the audience a different message.

Visual aids can also make your presentation more interactive. If you are going to use visual aids, provide only enough to serve as a guide to your speech. If you believe they can bring value to your presentation, then implement the use of technology, flip charts, whiteboards, handouts, and even magic. There is something to be said about illusions to enhance your message. Believe it or not, we even have a client who pairs magic with his message.

Positioning - Where Should You Stand?

Your position and the positioning of the visual aids are important. When you are presenting be sure to stand to the side of the screen to allow your audience an opportunity to see the slide. I would suggest that if you are in the Western Culture of the United States, consider standing to the left of your screen as people read from left to right and they simply like you more when you stand on the left side of the screen. Now, this would go to the opposite depending on what culture or part of the world you are in.

Remember that technology can improve the overall quality of your presentation in many ways. Tech is but just one aspect of the presentation. The other and most important factor is you. You are the voice the audience needs to be focused on. And your preparedness and presence of mind during the presentation are essential for that desired goal - for that successful presentation. Going on that stage or going into that presentation knowing that you've thoroughly prepared will boost your confidence. This will in turn enhance the quality of your presentation and strengthen your authority as the subject matter expert. Deliver your message in a way that only you can. Deliver with the right tools - with the right technology.

One of our clients, Melissa, was asked to be the keynote speaker for an upcoming conference. She was clearly a subject matter expert and a highly respected voice within her field. While she was extremely comfortable with speaking, she decided to work with DSB Leadership Group as she had never given a presentation to such a large group of professionals.

[79]

Talk It Up! - A Guide To Successful Public Speaking

After we learned about the amount of time she was allotted to speak, we worked with her to not only prepare a great presentation but also to help her with the technology she was incorporating into her presentation. We greatly reduced the number of slides she originally wanted to use. We also changed the color usage/template of the slides and reduced the 'noise' by minimizing what would be used on the slides themselves. She rehearsed until her comfort matched her confidence.

She crushed her presentation and received incredible comments and feedback. The result also led to receiving invitations to speak or be a featured speaker for other events. Sometimes a simple decluttering of a presentation can 'open up' the audience to fully grasp the presenter and their message.

Reflection
1. *What* has been your experience with integrating technology in your presentations?
2. *What* technology tool are you most interested in learning and willing to incorporate into your speaking 'toolbox'? Experiment and increase the experience with technology.

CHAPTER 11
Impromptu Talks

Have you ever been tapped on the shoulder or placed on the spot and asked to fill in or replace someone and speak? Many of us have been in that exact position where we needed to speak, and it was completely unexpected. What did you do? Did you find any success, or did you flame out? This scenario happens more often than you think. We are talking about impromptu speaking. This is speaking with little to no notice and with little to no preparation. They are typically centered around something you have some experience with or know something about.

Consider that potentially every conversation you have, including job market reviews and job interviews are, in a way, impromptu. That social event, meeting at work, or conference call has changed because the featured presenter somehow does not show up because they are either sick or stuck in traffic. Now you are on deck and asked to share. How about when your boss is asking for feedback and input and happens to look your way? Of course, being put on the spot, you have to say something.

How will that affect your career? How will that affect your psyche? Will you be discouraged? Would you be embarrassed? It can be a challenging position to be in and it can leave you feeling exposed as all eyes are now on you. We provided this section because we want you to approach these situations with confidence.

Do not be surprised when you are put on the spot or asked to deliver an impromptu speech. We want you to expect that you will be asked. My (David) mentor early in my ministry career shared that I should always be prepared. Trust me when I tell you that there have been countless times when I have been asked at the last minute to provide an update, share my thoughts, provide feedback, deliver a sermon, and believe it or not, officiate a wedding.

In an incredible article by Anett D. Grant and Amanda Taylor within the Business and Professional Communication Quarterly entitled, 'It's More Than Just Talk: Patterns of CEO Impromptu Communication[1]'. In the article, their research revealed that inducing rhetorical self-awareness helps to assess communication skills.[1] They also found that many CEOs express concern over impromptu speaking and that strategies including coaching greatly help.[1]

Talk It Up! - A Guide To Successful Public Speaking

Not so long after starting DSB Leadership Group, I (David) was in a scenario where this happened to me. It turned out to be my first meeting at a chamber that I had joined a week earlier. I showed up with only business cards and a pen. The COO of the Chamber asked if they could briefly speak with me. My initial thought was that they were going to welcome me as a new member, share some of the benefits of joining and perhaps direct me to some of the key professionals I should introduce myself to. Instead, they shared that they had only moments ago received a call from the chamber event's keynote speaker, and you can already surmise that they were unable to make it. They asked if it were possible for me to fill it as they noticed by my membership that I was a speaker. While I did not have any material or my laptop, I decided to say yes and was able to deliver a message. What helped was that the previous day, I was the keynote speaker for another event. I modified my message to fit within the 25-minute allotment. That is still one of my favorite keynote messages.

What if I had declined that invitation? What do you suppose would have happened to my brand and my credibility as a speaking coach and communications trainer? Believe it or not, this unexpected moment has led to my reputation growing and to new clients. You never know what could be awaiting you should you be able to 'drive in the winning run' as a pinch hitter in the bottom of the ninth in the seventh game of the World Series[2].

The next time you are put on notice or asked to give an impromptu presentation, do not fret over it. Set yourself up to drive in the winning run or hit a 'grand slam'[3]. Be the hero and be ready to speak in a pinch.

Smile, Center, & Go
Here are some things you can keep in mind when asked to share at a moment's notice: smile, center, and go!

- *Smile* - never look surprised or nervous, but excited to be presented with an opportunity to speak and strengthen leadership's belief in your ability to deliver.
- *Center yourself* - calm your mind, concentrate on your body, and breathe. This will allow you to think freely and give you a moment to collect your thoughts. Remember the power of the pause. Stand or sit up straight and project your voice with confidence.
- *Go* - This goes without saying that if you prepare for these moments, then these will be a 'piece of cake'. Do not apologize or give yourself an out by conveying a sense of insecurity. If you are nervous, others will be sure to follow you and be nervous as well. You will do an excellent job and will represent yourself and your organization well.

[82]

Talk It Up! - A Guide To Successful Public Speaking

A Few Techniques

Keep in mind that your response or speech should contain an introduction (set the scene), have a body (content), and then a conclusion. Consider the following techniques while drafting an outline either in your mind or on paper:

1. *Point, Reason, Illustration, Point*
2. *Compare & Contrast*
3. *Pros & Cons*

1.   Point, Reason, Illustration, & Point (PRIP).

Begin your speech or presentation by making a point. Make the point simple and clear. This could be an opportunity to make it memorable. It must relate directly to the reason why you were asked to speak. After making a point, provide a Reason for why you made that point. Next, share an illustration(s) to support that point. This can be done through a story, practical examples, and statistics. Lastly, conclude with that point you made at the beginning. This is simple and easy to follow.

The number of points or PRIPs you will be making will be determined by the amount of time you are given. We recommend that you keep in mind the 'Rule of 3'. Look at Chapter 4 for more insight into why we encourage the 'Rule of 3'.

You may not have much time to prepare before taking that 'stage'. Therefore, it's called impromptu speaking. Keep it simple and lean on your experience and knowledge. If you have done your homework and prepared for these moments, then you will not only crush it, but you will also come across as someone who's confident and as someone who is a person of authority. And, from that time with you, everyone will walk away with something memorable.

2.   Compare & Contrast

Compare and contrast or before and after is another technique that allows you to paint a picture and show progress or regression to support your point or message. Speak from what you know to be true and only share specific numbers or data points if they are accurate. You can be sure someone will 'fact check' you should you go down that path. This technique can be used to inspire or invoke emotion and potentially action.

Consider the power of change and growth: personally, professionally, and organizationally. We all love to hear about the person who overcame and defied the odds. We love to hear about the startup that grew to challenge the giants of the industry. Here is another tip we encourage leadership to consider implementing when speaking: talk about your people and their contributions as

[83]

Talk It Up! - A Guide To Successful Public Speaking

these lead to the growth and overall success of the company. Never be shy with your praise.

Don't forget a summary at the very end to wrap up the impromptu with a 'bow'.

3. Pros & Cons

This technique allows you to address the pros first before listing any of the cons which will reflect growth or the benefits of learning or choosing a certain perspective. Afterward, you can provide a summary and clearly state what your recommendation would be.

Give the pros for why some position you want to present should be right or should be accepted or should be the one that everybody buys into. Secondly, you want to give the cons. What did or what are the reasons why it may not work.

Here is a scenario; you are in a business meeting with an incredible opportunity and are asked to share a few thoughts - thoughts that will get the audience or prospect to lean your way and sign on the dotted line. Why should they go with you and not with someone else? You can thank your boss later for putting you on the spot; even better when he thanks you for closing the deal that puts your team over the quota.

Be confident and give the pros for why. More state that they 'bought' because of the confidence of the salesperson and not necessarily because of the product or solution itself. You thoroughly know your product or service and so this is a piece of cake. Present the pros of why you (they choose you first) and your product or service is the right solution. Then give your cons. This could be the 'short-term satisfaction, long-term disappointment'. This could be the 'horror' story of how those who did not initially choose you, came back to you. The cons should paint the picture of saving them the heartache and pain.

We train executives on how this technique can be particularly effective when speaking to the C-Suite or Executive Level Management Group. Speak their language and use their numbers as people and organizations never argue against their own numbers. You do not want to come across as someone who talks negatively about their organization. Making them feel bad about their leadership will not work in securing a deal. Praise and elevate their great qualities and tie in with the pros of your speech how this will equate to honoring or complementing those qualities.

The pros show how this is going to benefit them and the company. Then you wrap it up. Your position should be the one everybody walks away with.

[84]

Talk It Up! - A Guide To Successful Public Speaking

Giving A Toast

You are at a wedding and have been asked to speak and share a few words. This is customary for the Best Man, Maid, or Matron of Honor to do. You have likely heard your share of terrible and embarrassing speeches that made you wonder why this tradition continues. But from time to time, you might hear one that instantly becomes a classic as it moves everyone at the reception.

The reason why so many go awry is that they are either: never prepared and delivered 'by the cuff', poorly written, sprinkled with an awkward sense of humor, or presented with a 'flair' about themselves and not the actual Bride or Groom.

Here is a thought that goes without saying, if you practice and prepare, then you can expect the speech to go well.

Using A Microphone

If you are presented with a handheld microphone, then make sure to take the microphone firmly in your hand. You may want to consider taking the microphone initially with both hands to ensure you do not drop it. Use a firm grip and do not fidget with the handheld microphone as this could lead to it being dropped or to a poor and inconsistent sound.

Remember that the microphone is there to amplify sound - amplify your voice. Please do not do what so many do when they tap the mic with their hands or ask if 'everyone can hear' you. Trust that the sound and technical crew are doing their job and hold the mic about six to eight inches away from your mouth. Any closer and the room will hear you breathing; any further away and the room will have a difficult time hearing that wonderful speech. Let's not forget to check if the handheld is on and has batteries (if wireless).

If you are presented or asked to speak into a fixed or stationary microphone, know that the rules are remarkably like those of using the handheld mic. The distance of six to eight inches may now become eight to ten inches. Please note that you do not need to grab or adjust the microphone. If any adjustment needs to be made due to the height of the speaker, then look to adjust the 'neck' and not the microphone itself. The technical crew should have the sound and volume adjusted already and will not need you to 'test' the microphone. Take a moment to, at the minimum, see if the microphone is on or turned to the on position.

[85]

Talk It Up! - A Guide To Successful Public Speaking

If being asked to work with a wireless headset, then know that you are speaking what is known as 'hands-free'. You should not have to adjust or touch the headset. Your hands are free to support your speaking.

In using a lavalier (also known as a lapel) microphone, note that you should not have to adjust the microphone once it has been attached or clipped onto your clothing. Prior to use, the lavalier mic should be tested and fully charged or fitted with new batteries.

Here is a good rule of thumb: know how to turn the microphone on and off, or on and pause. The last thing you want is to forget that the microphone is 'still on' or on when you least expect it, i.e., being in the bathroom or while you are engaged in a private conversation. Trust us, the world does not need to hear about those activities.

Here Are Some Additional Reminders

- *Practice regularly.* Consider the moments when you could be asked and the types of questions or topics you might be presented with. While you may not be able to necessarily practice for a specific speech; you can practice how to respond and deliver a thought or speech with confidence.
- *Think before you speak.* Our mother used to say that "you should think before you speak". Once something leaves your mouth, you cannot take it back. Remember the power of the pause. You likely know enough to speak on the topic or subject you are being asked to cover. The challenge is that when you do not formulate your thoughts, you tend to ramble on or come across as not being confident.
- *Repeat the question.* There is a good chance that there are others who did not hear the question being asked. Repeating the question not only ensures that the audience knows what you are responding to; it also gives you that split moment to formulate your thoughts and response. Don't rush this as it will be appreciated and received as you are being thoughtful.
- *When in doubt, leave it out.* If you don't know something and then begin to 'fake it till you make it', don't be surprised should an audience member or subject matter expert push back or question you. Tell yourself that you may not have an answer at that moment, and you will avoid this trap of needing to have 'the answer' and not just an answer. You can always get back to that person or get back to them with a response. If you choose to say this, then make sure you actually get back to them.
- *Forgetting or fabricating responses* could damage your reputation and hurt your own professional advancement. Find a way to state or share what you know. You can also begin with, "I have heard" or "from what I have seen".

[86]

Talk It Up! - A Guide To Successful Public Speaking

- *Illustrations and storytelling can prove helpful* in supporting your position during a Q&A period.
- *Trust the lead or the moderator (if present).* They will usually guide the discussion or Q&A period and move the period along.
- *Remember that it's about the audience.* What do they need to hear from you? You can also engage the audience with a 'consider this' statement or question, by asking for a volunteer or with a Q & A session (we will cover more of this later).
- *Be mindful of the time.* You do not want to get carried away and lose the trust of those depending on you to deliver a concrete and confident message. Short and simple is usually best. If you have done your presentation justice, then naturally you can expect curiosity, questions, and more interest in you and your presentation.

The Breakdown

Here is an example of how to break down your impromptu speech or response. If you are working with a two-minute response, then break it down into a 20-30 second introduction, a 60-70 second body (content), and then a 20-30 conclusion. You can also provide a call to action at the very end. If you are working with a five-minute window, then consider lengthening the main body or content of the response or speech. Keep the introduction about the same length as you would with a two-minute response.

Remember to stay confident and to speak with passion and conviction. Do not be nervous. Be authentic. They will be gracious and appreciate your willingness to fill in and lead the discussion. We often share in our workshops that we should see the audience as incredible supporters. They want you to be successful because they don't want this to be a waste of their time either.

Consider These Possible Introductions To An Impromptu Speech

- "I know that John's not here. I know that Mary's not here. And I appreciate you giving me the confidence and the attention to share a couple of thoughts. What I am going to share is only a snippet of the information you would receive from John or Mary, and we will make sure that gets in your hands".

Or jump straight in without an 'explanation'.

- "I appreciate the chemistry of our team and believe that you will be (insert the objective such as encouraged, inspired, or convinced)". Recall one of the techniques and remember that less is more. Keeping it simple is always best.

[87]

Talk It Up! - A Guide To Successful Public Speaking

It pains us when we hear stories from professionals and executives who begin by talking down about themselves or when they take self-deprecation to the 'extreme'. You cannot be the focus and hope for sympathy should you bomb that opportunity. Be the infighter and continue the flame of excitement and strengthen the belief or buy in with your speech.

These techniques are quite simple and easy to use when supporting your goal of delivering a successful impromptu speech. Be prepared by practicing and knowing your 'material'. Our advice would be to always be ready as you never know when you might have to pinch-hit or go in to save the day.

A word of caution, if you do not know, don't pretend you do. As we stated earlier, there may be that one person who knows all the facts, stats, history, and industry. Do not jeopardize your reputation and hurt your credibility by not having the discipline to control what comes out of your mouth. There will be no walk of shame but stepping stones toward the walk of fame when you deliver with confidence. You will become a relied upon resource. Being dependable makes you invaluable.

The audience is not to be feared. Believe that they want you to be successful in delivering that impromptu speech. They do not want to see that time with you speaking as a wasted time out of their schedule. So, when you are put on the spot, do not be overcome with anxiety. Give graciously to your listeners and they will be gracious to you. You are there to give. They are there to receive. They are going to applaud you for your courage. They are going to salute you for your willingness to get up because they did not want to do it.

Be yourself, hold true to your 'batting stance', and have some fun with it. Remember that you are awesome. If you don't feel you delivered a great impromptu, do not run away from these in the future. Prepare, practice, and anticipate more opportunities to get back up to the plate and have another swing.

Activity
1. *List* out the scenarios where you might be asked to speak and practice how you might best respond to them.
2. *Which* of the strategies listed above naturally fit for those situations and around your own strengths and your own batting stance?
3. *Schedule* a time this week to have friends and or colleagues put you on the spot and ask you questions.

CHAPTER 12
Handling Questions & Awards

Your presentation is over and now you are about to be peppered with a ton of questions. Are you ready for them? Should you be concerned? What should your thought process be with handling any questions or feedback? Should you become defensive and view these as a threat or a challenge to you and your knowledge? Should you give a direct response or try a technique such as answering their question with a question? Is there a benefit to pausing and using that moment to collect your thoughts? You prepared for a presentation; do you now need to prepare for questions? Did you notice the number of questions presented in this first paragraph?

How you respond will reflect on you and your reputation can be damaged if you handle this opportunity poorly. Remember to be confident with your response. Be honest and never sugarcoat, minimize, or tell any type of 'white' lie no matter how innocent it may seem. It is more than okay to note that it is not wrong to disagree as they may be misinformed or confused. It is more than appropriate to 'push back'. Try saying, 'do you mind if I push back or challenge that?'

Here are some things to keep in mind should you ever find yourself in a situation where you have time for questions or feedback or are being asked to respond to the audience.

1. **Accept Questions & Feedback**
Do not be nervous or become anxious at the thought of what to do with that moment following your presentation. Questions can be a sign of interest. If your audience is interested in your topic and presentation, you can expect questions from an engaged audience. They may simply be curious and want clarification or they may desire more information on something you shared. We view questions as a great opportunity as this can further connect you with your listeners and strengthen your brand.

There will be the occasional dissent, where they cannot be satisfied. We will address this with tip number four but believe in yourself and in your message. Your ability to stay level-headed and not giving in to emotion may make all the difference. This could lead the rest of the audience to show their disapproval of that objective voice.

Talk It Up! - A Guide To Successful Public Speaking

You can also ask questions yourself to get clarification. You want to make sure you are addressing the concerns and not adding any "fuel" to the fire or adding new objections.

Not all questions or comments will be there to 'build or fluff your ego'. Some of the questions may indeed be difficult to address or answer. Should you encounter something that was not something you addressed or covered during your speech or presentation; it is worth mentioning that the question being asked of you was not something you covered in that presentation. You may also mention covering it in a future presentation or that you will make a note to get back to them.

2. Pause & Address

Breathe - take a deep breath and gather your thoughts. Remember the power of the pause. Pausing even for a brief moment will provide you with the necessary time to consider an appropriate response. There is even within the pause a technique that we encourage you to consider. This is a technique that will convey a depth of communication and one that will reflect your strength of listening. Repeat the question back to confirm that you understand what is being asked. Repeating the question again will allow for the entire room/rest of the audience to hear what was asked before you provide a response. Here is a technique you may want to consider: try paraphrasing their question to make it align with your position and then respond. The key here is that context matters.

There is an old adage that 'there is no such thing as a silly question'. So, use this to show how valid their question is. Be sincere about this and you will not damage your credibility. You can even try saying something like:

- "I appreciate that question as it is one that I often receive."
- "That is a great question, thank you for asking."
- "That is a point we've been discussing as well."
- "That is very interesting and one that I will need to think about."

After responding you may also want to consider asking:

- "Does that answer your question"?
- "Can I provide more insight or information"?

When you pause, you also provide the individual who is asking the question the opportunity to completely ask their question. We see far too often responses to incomplete questions. There is a scripture from the *Holy Bible* in the book of *James* that says, "everyone should be quick to listen, slow to speak and slow to become angry" (*James 1:19*). Giving them the 'floor' will convey that you are taking that time to consider their question and validate that what they are asking is important.

[90]

As mentioned, pausing gives you time to think about an appropriate response, and afterward, you will be able to deliver that response with clarity and eloquence.

3.   Make Eye Contact & Smile
It is especially important, when possible, to make eye contact with the individual who asked the question. Gauge the atmosphere of the room to determine if you should keep your attention on the one who posed the question or if it would be best served to also engage the entire room. Eye contact shows a presenter is engaged and not someone who will easily write off the person asking the question.

There are few speakers and leaders who have the incredible ability to make you feel like you are the only one in the room. The main technique to create this atmosphere is eye contact. The second is to use their name by thanking them for asking the question or by using their name somewhere within your response.

There is something magical about a smile. Do not be stingy with them as they can be inviting and express appreciation and even help to guide the remaining questions from that moment forward. Don't be surprised by 'the oxygen' given to the 'flame' of the moment. This could be both a positive working in your favor and a negative, leading you to want to leave the stage. Remember that fire can be a good tool, but it must be controlled.

4.   Remain Calm
Remain calm and remember that you are in control. Don't give this up. You are the one with the microphone and you can direct questioning in a way that would best serve you and the entire audience.

Never make it a debate. Remember that buyers never argue with their own data, numbers, or position. Interrupting or arguing with them leaves you little to no room for closing the deal. It will likely leave you losing that opportunity.

Never get angry or at the very least, never show that you are frustrated. Anger is what will be remembered, and your message no matter how good may be forgotten. Lasting impressions matter, so stay cool no matter what arises. You can always ask them to hold their questions and say you will get back to them. Let them know that you appreciate their: time, the question, professionalism, or the passion behind their question. Direct the questions toward what you delivered or covered and nothing else. Make a conscious effort to stay away from 'triggers' such as politics/geopolitics.

Hopefully, you will never have to encounter a heckler or someone who comes across as being insensitive or rude when you are speaking but be prepared should one ever-present themselves. They care little about embarrassing themselves and want the presenter to be caught off guard. The audience will be

[91]

Talk It Up! - A Guide To Successful Public Speaking

just as disappointed as you are with this disrespectful disrupter. There may be an issue in their life and not an issue with you or your presentation.

Use the line that works for me 'if you want to speak briefly afterward, I would be happy to'. Ask them to hold their comments and thoughts until the very end. As the saying goes, 'kill them with kindness'. Staying calm will usually deter the heckler away. Kill them with kindness. Say, thank you, and then get back to your focus. The event organizer should also be on alert and assist the heckler out of the room and conference.

I (David) remember that there was a particular incident where an individual wanted to berate and make a scene while I was delivering a presentation. When there was no getting through to this person, I calmly said that I would be happy to meet with him to fully hear him out after the presentation. I made an appeal to his better nature and mentioned that there were other people in the auditorium who wanted to hear what was being shared. He obliged and we were able to speak after. He was clearly frustrated and being able to feel like I cared was enough to calm him down. He had no specific issues with me or the content of my presentation but felt as if he was not being heard by the event organizers and the sponsoring organization. I was able to facilitate a discussion with that person and the event organizer.

Perhaps they are legitimately frustrated or even intoxicated. Take control! You establish the rules. I encourage you to practice responding and not react to potentially toxic people or questions that will not serve the audience.

Consider watching online videos of how President Obama or other well-reputed speakers handle these situations.

5. Be Honest
If you don't know, say that you don't know. There may be times when you are being presented with questions that you just don't know the answer to. It would be wise to not pretend to know the answer. Be honest and say that you don't know the answer. This is not a time to bluff or pretend as there actually may be someone in the audience who does know the answer, and this could hurt your reputation and even undermine your confidence. Let them know that you will get back to them, and you better get back to them.

Temperature Check
Your responses to questions being asked can go a long way to strengthening your brand, position, and reputation. Get the audience on your side by being gracious and by delivering thoughtful responses.

Talk It Up! - A Guide To Successful Public Speaking

Consider doing a temperature check by asking if your answer addressed their question - if you provided a satisfactory response. You can also gauge the room by listening to the questions being asked. If they naturally follow each other with similar questions around a specific topic or aspect of your presentation, then you can prepare your responses accordingly. This will continue to build excitement and appreciation for you and your work.

Keys To Remember

1. *Know* your subject, material, services, and/or products - know your brand. Speak from a position of strength as you are the subject matter expert.
2. *Accept* that you may have those who won't be receptive to your message. Accept that you won't make everybody happy, so stop making this your goal. I (David) early in my career spoke before an audience of 2,000 at Constitution Hall in Washington, DC. Although it seemed like a fantastic presentation, I walked out feeling disappointed, thinking that I had failed to move all 2,000 people. I credit my mentor Steve Cannon who helped me to see my role as a speaker from a different perspective - using different lenses.

   That is a life that has been impacted and forever changed. The adage or quote by John Lydgate is true, "Yes, you can please some of the people all of the time, you can please all of the people some of the time, but you can't please all of the people all of the time.[1]"

   He helped me to identify what the goal of my speaking was. He identified that if one person walked away from my speech impacted, inspired, and gained perspective; then I have done an incredible job. He reminded me that I was there to graciously give. It may take some time after hearing a speaker for more people to change. It could take conversations 'offline', with attendees sharing with each other, that the message takes root and leads to your initial goal as a speaker.

3. *Research* demographics of the buyer and their organization: personalities, industry, etc. Do not go 'guns a blazing' and be aggressive. Understand their language and take time to research and learn about the various behavioral models.
4. *Listen* to understand versus listening to respond. Listening could be the topic of its own book. There is incredible value as a speaker if you could master critical listening skills. Listening to understand instead of listening to react (make your point) takes incredible discipline and sympathy. This trait can make all the difference in winning your audience.

[93]

Talk It Up! - A Guide To Successful Public Speaking

Acceptance Speeches

How do you handle praise? This can speak as much as your presentation does about who you are and your character.

Applause is one of the most common compliments anyone can receive, and you can be sure that one can be tested by their own reaction to the praise they receive. How long do they clap for? Do they stand up? Do they vocally cheer?

Fight the temptation to discount or deflect compliments. Your reputation can be at stake. Careful or you may engage in self-praise and give into arrogance. Show a little modesty. It is an honor to be recognized.

Why do we feel the need to say something other than 'thank you'?

So many think of acceptance speeches that you see from the Emmys, Oscars, or Grammy winners and believe that is what you should model your acceptance speech from. It may not be appropriate to thank everybody in your life, in your department, in your neighborhood, your dog walker, your gardener - you get the point. We have all seen lousy speeches. We have all seen boring speeches. Focus instead on the audience and consider the people and organizations that you truly need to thank - those who have been most instrumental toward you achieving that award or acknowledgment. Do it in a genuine and sincere way. Here is a tip, if those individuals are in the room, then look at them when you thank them. Say exactly what you are thankful for but keep it brief and precise. You must be mindful of the time you have to speak. If you are thanking only one or a few, then this may allow for you to not only share specifically why or how they supported you; but you can add a short story to paint that picture.

Speaking of stories, you can share a short story relating to the award itself. Consider trying the 'before and after' technique and how you overcame or were able to work through some challenge, and then you can tie in those you want to thank within that story. Try to avoid reading from a script or notecard as this can seem rehearsed and lack that authenticity. You want to be genuine and only use a note card to ensure you leave no one out. Do not read from it directly.

Accepting Awards & Compliments

Accepting awards should be met with the same element of gratitude and grace. Here are some helpful thoughts on what to know before accepting an award, certificate, or compliment.

- *Establish* with the event planner or organizer the protocol or expectations of responses. Should one be necessary, please clearly state parameters

Talk It Up! - A Guide To Successful Public Speaking

including the amount of time being provided to share a response or give an acceptance speech.

- *If* you are not given much time, you can never go wrong with a smile and a simple 'thank you'. You can even add, 'I appreciate this'. Whatever the award or compliment, graciously accept them.
- *If* you are expected to or are given 'the floor' to provide an acceptance speech, remember your own 'batting stance'. Your acceptance speech should be personal and heartfelt.
- *Be* gracious and gracefully accept the compliment. Accepting can be as simple as 'smiling' and saying, 'thank you'. Careful not to downplay the compliment to come across as being humble. For example, someone says that they have never heard that topic spoken of in that manner before or that it was the greatest they have ever heard. Only to have you respond with, 'it was nothing, anyone could have said the same thing'.
- *Use* wisdom with accepting the compliment and take care not to deflect or turn it back on the person or group complimenting or praising you. For example, after receiving praise or an acknowledgment, you turn it around by saying something to the effect of 'they are also a great speaker' or 'anyone could have done this'. Not accepting the compliment can come across as being rude, conceited, condescending, and lacking empathy. You are shifting from allowing them the right to say something nice.
- *Be* gracious and humble. Acknowledge the work by others including the organization and leadership that selected you for the award. You can even consider adding an appropriate message to inspire or encourage. For example, "I humbly accept this award on behalf of all..." These could be those unsung heroes, your peers, your parents, etc. You could even add something as simple as 'you are the real inspiration'.
- *Show* excitement. It is an honor to be recognized for who you are. It is incredible that your work is accepted and appreciated, so never show disappointment, or have your face reflect that this honor is 'not a big deal'. You will be amazed by how much your face reflects your emotions. Recall our thoughts on this within the section on body language in Chapter 2.
- *Practice,* practice, and then practice. This cannot be overstated, and you have seen this point throughout this book. Practice does indeed make better! Your response may make an incredible impression on those who may have the ability to 'pull strings' and 'make the calls' toward even greater opportunities.
- *Note* ahead of time who the event organizer is and how you should enter and leave the stage after receiving your award.

Presenting An Award

Should you be in a position where you will be the person delivering or presenting an award, here are some things to keep in mind:

[95]

Talk It Up! - A Guide To Successful Public Speaking

- *Prepare* what you want to say ahead of time and then practice, practice, and practice. This cannot be overstated.
- *Use* your position wisely and do not make this about you but keep it simple and direct the attention to the awardee. Keep your introduction brief. You may introduce yourself and thank the organization for asking you to present.
- *State* the name of the award itself and briefly describe what the award is for. Consider including if this is a local, regional, national, or international award. You can explain what the recipient of the award did to receive the honor. Consider the parameters used to select the awardee including any causes they represented. Present the picture.
- *Acknowledge* those in the room who were also considered for the award. Keep it brief and always be mindful of the time. Remember that this is about the awardee.
- *Build* excitement and consider that in many situations, not many will know who the recipient of the award will be. The excitement should continue up until the award is presented.
- *Try* to avoid unnecessary stories and being humorous if this is not your strength or batting stance.

Gifts & Giveaways

We are often asked if there should be gifts or giveaways for the audience. While it may not be expected, there will be moments where a gift or giveaway may add to your presence and time with the audience. Many speakers will give out marketing pieces, some of their books, links for free eBooks, materials, or even gift certificates. Should you do this, consider employing some creativity. You can show this by either taping a card on the bottom of some random chairs, by randomly drawing names, or by presenting those gifts and giveaways to those who ask quality questions during your Q&A.

I (David) during a presentation as the keynote speaker asked if there were any who followed the Twins Talk it Up podcast. If you are curious, he did not ask the audience to raise their hand. He followed that initial question by asking if they learned from the most recent Twins Talk it Up episode how Danny had received his nickname. There were a few who at this time raised their hand to respond. The prize was either a free executive coaching session or access at no cost to a DSB Leadership Group course. Do you know what Danny's nickname is and how he received it? Go to YouTube or your favorite Podcast platform, subscribe and download to learn. Once you do, you will refer to him by this nickname.

Activity

1. *Create* and keep response handling flashcards or scripts available. Response and talking points cards will aide in keeping you focused and in control.

2. *Write* out possible questions and responses to those questions.

3. *Schedule* time this week to practice and role play with a colleague on how you would respond to commonly asked questions or possible scenarios, which should reflect your industry and be appropriate and reflect properly on your products, services, and or company.

Conclusion

Speak confidently on any stage. This one skill set can be the difference-maker and empower your life, both personally and professionally. You have a message, and they need to hear it. Remember what's at stake? They won't receive the heart of the message - your heart - because they miss being able to hear from you.

We know you will experience great growth because of believing in yourself and by getting out there and using the skills you have gained. There is no greater teacher than experience; so, put in the time and keep speaking. Find your own 'batting stance' and stay true to your authentic voice and you will indeed connect on a heart level and influence the masses.

So, don't try to be perfect. The audience connects with imperfections or should we say reality. We are not perfect, but we can be courageous and take action. Good luck and reach out to our team here at DSB Leadership Group for Advanced Speaking Training and other tools to support your professional growth.

David Suk Brown & Danny Suk Brown

WORKSHOP 1
Imposter Syndrome

Feelings of not being worthy or deserving can be seen as having an inferiority complex. This is also known as Imposter Syndrome. Imposter syndrome describes a phenomenon where, despite external evidence of their competence, people feel intrinsically unworthy of their success and are afraid others will eventually realize they don't deserve it.

So, it is having feelings of being a fraud. It's driven by a fear of being 'discovered or found out' as not being as smart or talented or deserving or experienced or (fill in the blank) as people think.

Evidence of this can be if you persistently feel like you are not good enough to be in the position that you are in, or even you are not good enough to be in the position that others are in. It is reflected in the idea that you have only succeeded because of luck or by chance and not because of your hard work, talent, or qualifications.

Growing up, I (David) was tempted to think this way. Every little brother looks up to his older brother and wants to be like him. I struggled with this and had to learn over time to be the best David I could be even if I could not be quite like my twin. This motivated me.

If you have ever had these feelings, you are not alone. According to a study published in the International Journal of Behavioral Science (entitled The Impostor Phenomenon), an estimated 70% of people experience these imposter feelings at some time in their lives.[1]

Even the great novelist Maya Angelou once said, "I have written eleven books, but each time I think, uh oh, they're going to find out now. I've run a game on everybody, and they're going to find me out."[2] Usually, high achievers and perfectionists are most tempted to struggle with this complex. Got to know everything before saying anything. Even knowing 99% leaves them insecure. Asking for help makes them feel like an incapable leader and a fraud. They'd rather be Superman[3] and hope no one identifies their kryptonite[3].

Do any of these statements sound familiar?

- I did not imagine I would win that contract with my proposal. I wonder if they will regret awarding it to me.

Talk It Up! - A Guide To Successful Public Speaking

- To my surprise, I got the position (or promotion). How long until they realize it was a mistake?
- You're delivering a presentation, and the one thing going through your mind, over and over, is the feeling that you don't belong up there. It's hard to focus on your talking points; you're too preoccupied by the fear that you don't really know what you're talking about, and once the audience asks you a question, they'll all see how full of it you are.

Can you experience this imposter feeling at your workplace? While at work, you literally go in every day waiting for someone to approach you or call you into their office and say something to the effect of 'you do not know what you are doing'.

Even in my relationships, it is so difficult to be close or to get close to someone and open up. I never feel comfortable because what if they are not seeing the real me and what they like is actually fake?

If you have ever struggled with the fear of being unmasked as an imposter, here are some suggestions that may be of assistance:

1. Reframing

Reframe your thinking. Acknowledge those thoughts and put them into perspective. The True Imposter here is not you; the imposter is Fear. Fear is not real. It is a projection of something that has not yet happened. Why experience the potentially damaging effects of an event that has not yet happened twice. There is a difference between fear and danger. Stop thinking like an imposter to stop feeling like one!

- **Exercise:** Affirmation Statements
- **Exercise:** Separate feelings from facts and write a new script
- **Exercise:** Gratitude Journal/Victory Journal

Be driven as a leader but go about it with grace. Permission to make mistakes and to forgive yourself. Learn from your weaknesses and mistakes. This is healthy and a great place to learn instead of a place to beat yourself up.

- **Exercise:** Power of visualization. Visualize what success looks like.

2. Own Your Success

Own your successes and achievements. Do not minimize nor discard your work and efforts. You worked hard to be where you are. Do the first 2 on this list and imagine where you could be. You can still be both humble and the hero of your story.

It's not luck or a fortunate moment. Jodi Foster when she won her Oscar infamously said, "I thought it was a fluke".

Talk It Up! - A Guide To Successful Public Speaking

- **Exercise:** Gratitude Journal/Victory Journal. Write in this journal daily and look back during those moments when you are tempted to think less of yourself.

3. Don't Compare

Don't fall for the trap of comparing yourself to others. This is not always an 'apples to apples' comparison. You are unique. It is not fair nor right to make comparisons where you take your weaknesses versus others' strengths. Make the most of your gifts, talents, and hard work.

4. Don't Play It Safe

Now is the time for even greater risks. You may never know what you are capable of unless you try. Gamble on yourself as this brings about the greatest opportunities for growth. Each time you fall, you get back up and learn from that experience.

Discover and strengthen your own personal brand.

Consider

Brene Brown, when she developed the '5 Second Rule[4]'. It is her strategy to take action and defeat self-doubt.

Nike's slogan of "Just Do It"[5].

Think about the Movie 'Secret to my Success' with Michael J. Fox[6]. He knew he could be found out but did it anyway. His drive for success outweighed his thoughts of being caught; by his thoughts of being exposed. He knew he was talented and deserved an opportunity to make that dream of his a reality.

5. Redefine Your Purpose - Start With Why By Simon Sinek[7]

Be fueled by your passion to live out your Why. In his book *Start with Why*, Simon Sinek through his 'Golden Circle' model explains how incredible leaders including Martin Luther King, Jr., and organizations like Apple have shifted minds and the landscape of buying because they were clear about their Why. Every person and every organization operates on three levels (Golden Circle): What we do, How we do it, Why we do it. Do you know your Why and can you articulate that?

6. Connectivity

It is important and strategic to stay connected with key relationships and partnerships. Stay open and honest with them. This leads to positive, meaningful, and even social relationships, where accepting feedback is helpful because you are in a 'safe zone'. Within this zone, there is no shame or silence. This is not a place to feed any feelings of inadequacy.

[103]

Talk It Up! - A Guide To Successful Public Speaking

Who do you know or who would you identify as someone who is authentic? These are the people who "speak their mind", who seem comfortable with 'their own skin' and are not easily embarrassed as they can make fun of themselves. They are not afraid to be wrong.

Remain connected to positivity and maintain partnerships that will encourage success and help you win. Consider some of the greatest sports dynasties, like the Chicago Bulls and their Championship runs. Michael Jordan would not allow his team to lose. He would not allow them to not believe that they would win. They found a way, because winning was the only option.

Mentoring and Coaching. This is key. Mentors and coaches can help confront feelings of fraudulent talk, help reframe negativity, and keep one on course to achieve greater goals.

Connect with yourself. Meditation, reflection, and even connection with and through nature. That hiking trail is vital, not because of conquering a hill, but to conquer yourself.

7. Vulnerability
I gather that the main underlying issue with imposter syndrome lies with vulnerability.

We mentioned reframing as a technique for combating imposter syndrome. We also would like to add that we should shift and reframe what it means to be vulnerable.

Dr. Tara Swart, a neuroscientist stated that those who have or struggle with imposter syndrome have underestimated the importance of a sense of belonging. Dr. Swart is quoted as saying, "What keeps our brains healthy and the basic need of the sense of belonging are exactly the same factors that neuroscience relates to what we call successful aging. Things such as rest, fuel, hydrate, oxygenate and simplify your life. Meaningful relationships. Connect regularly - and even on an emotional level (eating, coffee, etc.). Even connecting to nature feeds the brain."[8]

There is a questionnaire developed by Pauline Clance called the 'Clance IP Scale'[9]. There are 20 questions that upon completion will give you a sense of if you have imposter syndrome characteristics. You can find a link to this in the endnotes as well as in the additional resources section of this book.

As human beings, we are all imperfect. We put too much pressure on ourselves to be perfect instead of striving to be a better version of ourselves-better than the day before. Support yourself more than you criticize yourself. Listen to the inner coach and not the inner critic. You are still on the learning curve. Be kind and gracious to yourself. Be you! When you accept how incredible you are, you

[104]

Talk It Up! - A Guide To Successful Public Speaking

will not be haunted by this feeling of inadequacy. Instead, you will grow into the person you know you are.

Activity
- Download and listen to the Twins Talk it Up Podcast Episode 16: Conquering Imposter Syndrome[10]:
  https://www.youtube.com/watch?v=swJg2eX_ZCI

WORKSHOP 2
What Pros Do And Don't Do

What do professional speakers do well? What is it they do that the average speaker or presenter does not? What do they habitually avoid that others mistakenly do? What can you learn from these incredible speakers?

Professionals never state they will be done in a blank number of minutes nor that they are wrapping up their presentation. Doing this will draw your audience to concentrate or think about their watches, what they are having for lunch, or the email they need to follow up with, instead of the strong conclusion or crux of your message. Never say that you are 'almost done'.

These effective speakers command the room. They walk with purpose and never pace about. They speak to the entire room and not just to the 'smiling faces' or the faces smiling at them.

They often provide giveaways. These can include their books and gift cards. Try to avoid what every other presenter does by giving away useless junk or items that will eventually be thrown into the garbage. Placing your logo on something like this can hurt your brand.

Professional speakers have their own 'speaking personality' and do not try to be like someone else. Be authentic. Much like in the sport of baseball, you have your own batting stance. Be yourself. If you are not a completely funny person, then do not try to be a stand-up comedian. You do not need to be Tony Robbins, Jack Canfield, or Eric Thomas. You do not need to be a top booking motivational speaker. People will engage with you much more easily if you are honest, and act like yourself. Let your personality shine through.

People want to listen to people, they do not want to listen to monotone robots. So, be yourself, and let your personality show.

Professionals never put their hands in their pockets. They are completely aware of their body language. Believe it or not, you actually speak with your hands, and they can be incredible aids to your presentation. So, avoid putting your hands into your pockets and do not keep them stationary anywhere else on or around your body. This can be distracting and give the impression that you are not interested. Your audience may even mimic you and start putting their hands in their pockets. When you are using your hands in such a way, it will become distracting and give the impression that you are not interested.

Talk It Up! - A Guide To Successful Public Speaking

Use natural gestures - gestures that support what you are saying, and what your message is all about. Stay natural, stay positive and use hand gestures in a way that compliments what you say.

Unless you are a standup comedian, do not embarrass anyone in the room.

You do not want to call out anyone, embarrass anyone, or make a fool of anyone when you are giving a public speech. Know your audience. Keep it professional, even if you are giving the best man or maid/matron of honor speech.

This is a public arena, so be careful to be completely respectful of the podium and platform that you have. Calling someone out to embarrass them may backfire on you.

Professionals do not spend the time they have looking at the floor or at their notes (more on this to come). They engage the audience. They make eye contact. They are aware of their actions when they have 'the stage' and avoid looking down at the floor, at their feet, or at their notes. You want to use eye contact. Know your topic, know your speech, and engage with the audience. Draw them into what you are saying. Don't give them a reason to not be into you or your presentation.

They never and we mean never apologize. Do not say that you are nervous or not good at public speaking. Some self-depreciation is acceptable but drawing attention to yourself or apologizing for the obvious is not.

There is a time and a place to self-deprecate - to be modest. It is good to be secure in your own weaknesses and shortcomings and not be afraid to point them out when appropriate. Use this to support and empower your message. It is one thing to be transparent, and it is another to be falsely humble. You can run the risk of losing credibility before your audience, let alone lose your audience.

Do not call yourself out and say that you are not as good as you actually are, because people want you to succeed. People do not want to listen to someone who is going to completely fail. People are giving away their precious attention, and they want to give it to someone who is confident, and to someone who can deliver.

They do not read from their notes or directly from their presentation slides. They do not overly rely on technology as a crutch to aid their presentation.

If you are using a PowerPoint presentation, it is very important that you do not read from your slides. Your slides should not be your presentation but visual support. Relying on slides can bring the risk that your back will be turned away

[108]

from your audience. You could also isolate your audience by giving the impression that your attention to your slides is more important than they are. You have now just completely disengaged yourself because the focus is no longer on you but on something they could have received in an email.

Professionals do not use big or unfamiliar words. They are very mindful of the language and wording and will match or prepare according to their audience. They do not use words that won't connect with the audience. You can adjust the same presentation for different audiences.

Do not use big words unless it is absolutely necessary. Why go there? Do not assume they will follow you as they may be distracted trying to define the word(s) you have just said and not stay with your presentation. Know your audience and be mindful of acronyms, and industry lingo.

If you absolutely have to use big words, unfamiliar words, or acronyms, then make sure you define what that word or acronym means before you continue your speech. So, say the big word, define it, and then move on. Avoid technical jargon.

Make it simple. Remember that acronym KISS and 'Keep It Simple Silly'. Don't over-complicate your message and make sure it is relatable. You can take the same message and tailor it toward the demographic of your audience. Sometimes your brilliance can be heard in the simplicity of your delivery.

Even scientists use simple words or phrases to explain an idea, theory, or even an enormous number. For example, Astronomical Units or 'AU' are used to represent distances in space. One AU is the equivalent to approximately 93 Million Miles or 150 Kilometers.[1]

Professionals never on purpose show their nerves, or do they?

We do not want to draw unnecessary attention to anything that will not complement the message. Pacing back and forth like you are in a marching band will distract your audience. They will wonder why you are moving and behaving the way you are. Remember the adage of 'nervous energy' makes everyone else nervous. Be fluid with your movements.

Do not fidget with anything as this can also be seen as a nervous presenter. This includes pens, the pointer, or even your fingers. This may be unintentional and even unconscious, but it will do little to reflect who you are before your audience.

Another sign of speaking anxiety is when a presenter holds onto the lectern as if for 'dear life'. It won't save you. Use the stage or if you are confined, then

Talk It Up! - A Guide To Successful Public Speaking

learn to relax and you help your audience become comfortable and in a position to receive your message.

Try and be natural, as if you are having a conversation with your friend.

The professionals never look toward or for others to save them. If you have prepared properly, you will not need to have someone in the audience or on your team cover for you. Don't forget to practice, practice, and practice.

Bonus: Professionals use coaching from other professionals because they understand the value of having another 'set of eyes'. Do not forget to work with a speaking coach. A great coach may see and notice what you cannot, and they will bring out the best of you. They can also 'speed' up your development and mastery of this skill set.

Reflection
- *Take* these tips, review your own public speaking either on video or audio and see whether you are doing any of these things. Avoid these and you will become a better presenter and speaker. The key is to not look for every flaw or mistake. Instead, choose only one area at a time to improve. Feel free to generously give yourself praise for delivering your message how you intended for the message to be delivered. Don't hold back.

WORKSHOP 3
Your Elevator Pitch

Here's a situation that many professionals will find themselves in: you are at a networking event and are being asked to introduce yourself. What do you say? This is not the time to organize your thoughts. You must know what you are going to say, and you need to say it with confidence. This can be crucial as a first impression.

What is an elevator pitch and when is it used?

An elevator pitch traditionally is used to briefly introduce yourself, your company, or your organization. We believe that it is so much more than that. An elevator pitch is designed to get your audience to want more information. It is designed to get them to ask you to 'tell me more'.

An elevator pitch is not reserved for speaking only about your company, its products, and/or services. You could use them to present a new idea or concept to senior leadership such as your CEO. What about a new initiative for your team or department? Please adjust them to suit the audience. Your elevator pitch should have multiple variations pending your audience.

Tips For Your Elevator Pitch

- *Length* - A good elevator pitch should last no longer than a short elevator ride, hence the name. They should be no more than 30 seconds and must be both interesting and memorable. Practice to not come across as rushed or insecure.
- *Pinpoint the goal* - What is the outcome you are looking for with the elevator pitch? What do you want the audience to remember? How will what you say in that short time stand out from everyone else? If you are not thrilled with what you are going to say, then you should never expect your audience to be either.
- *Your Unique Selling Proposition (USP)* - What is your unique selling proposition? What is the unique service, product, or brand that sets you apart and makes you stand out? Your competitive edge reflects that one feature(s) will bring to light the benefits or value your customer base wants. Your USP can make all the difference when uniqueness is needed. Your company may already have a slogan or a brand that is easily recognizable, so the question lies in identifying who you are and what you

Talk It Up! - A Guide To Successful Public Speaking

do well. Use that tagline or slogan and tie it in with who you are as a representative of your company.

- **Structure**
  1. *Your name* (consider who are you, background, context)
  2. *Name* of company or organization you are representing
  3. *Your USP* (consider adding an interesting fact or statistic)
  4. *Make* the connection (consider an engaging question or something unexpected)
  5. *The Ask* (what do you want)
  6. *Your name*
  7. *Name* of company or organization you are representing
  8. *The close* or call to action (say thank you)
  9. *Optional slogan*

Test & Implement
Test it and then find what works best for each situation. Try it in front of your peers, focus group, or even friends. Keep in mind your tone, cadence, and body language fluidity.

Example - One Of David's Elevator Pitches
David Suk Brown, Speaking and Executive Coach with DSB Leadership Group. When you think of the greatest athletes and performers in the world, they all utilize coaching to get that winning edge. Could you use a winning edge? David Suk Brown, DSB Leadership Group, where we deliver that winning edge.

Talk It Up! - A Guide To Successful Public Speaking

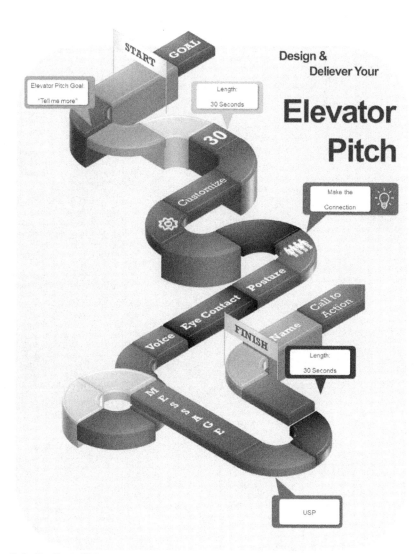

Design Your Elevator Pitch

[113]

WORKSHOP 4
Speaking With The C-Suite

Different communication skills are necessary for every level of leadership. There may be times when you will need to address or present to the Executive team, sometimes referred to as C-Suite. Although intimidating, this can bring you incredible success and help advance your career.

How should you present an idea? Should you challenge and offer a different perspective? How do you impress and prove your worth as an invaluable team member? You may have the best insight and the right solutions but none of this means anything if you are not a great communicator.

Here are seven things you need to communicate with the C-Suite:

1. Know The Players
Who are the key players? What do you know about the C-Suite members? What do you know about their roles? This will help you understand how senior executives communicate. What are their personality types? Are they straight to the point? Do they like data, facts, and illustrations?

Consider personality assessments such as DiSC[1] that will provide a focus on crafting conversation with those with whom you are speaking.

The Four DiSC Personality Types
- *D: DOMINANCE* - This style is both bold and skeptical.
- *i: INFLUENCE* - This style is both bold and accepting.
- *S: STEADINESS* - This style is both cautious and accepting.
- *C: CONSCIENTIOUSNESS* - This style is both cautious and skeptical.

Your message will be more effective and better received if you understand what is important to them. Think about the impact on the overall organization and not just your department (both positive and negative).

How many direct reports do they have? Are there any administrators or administrative assistants? Are they sticklers to their schedule? How do they like to be contacted/preferred method of contact? Is the reason for the conversation urgent? If it is not, then ask if an email would be appropriate. Emails should generally be short and straight to the point. The subject line of the email is key. Use bullet points and remember to be short and precise.

Talk It Up! - A Guide To Successful Public Speaking

What else would be key to know about the players?

2. Communicate Clearly & Communicate Often

Don't wait until the last minute to bring up an issue or concern. Don't wait until something bad happens. Emergencies can lead to panic and to you coming across as being demanding in your dialogue.

Frame your conversations as an opportunity for them and for the organization. Be comfortable and confident with what you are selling - yes, selling. You are always selling: an idea, position, or actual product and/or service.

Persist and do not give up but check your ego at the door. Persist and do not give up but check your ego at the door. There is a fine balance between confidence and awareness (humility). Your time is valuable and you must believe that you are worth their time. Have the awareness and humility to listen to and respect their time and their position. Never make assumptions.

3. Metrics & KPIs

Think like an executive and use metrics and more KPIs. KPIs or key performance indicators track whether you hit overall business objectives or targets and metrics track process.

In speaking with the members of the C-Suite or executive team, you need to have a firm grasp of the necessary metrics and KPIs. What are they? The appropriate data points used in a timely way will lead you to become viewed as a valued consultant and advisor. You may not have all the answers but you will get the right solution.

What metrics are you being measured by?

OKRs (Objectives & Key Results) - connecting company, team, and personal objectives. Objectives are the long-term goals and the key results are how you accomplish those goals.

Do you have a firm understanding of the overall objective of the organization? How do they measure growth and progress? If you want a green light or approval, then know what they want out of it. Paint a picture of the overall desired result! Show the Return on Investment (ROI), increased profitability, productivity, and the risks and potential loss of taking no action.

In the meeting, be prepared with these numbers - stats, history, and proper reasoning. Example: We can reduce the budget by $x\%$ versus I need $\$x$ to buy more hardware. Being proactive versus reactive. The higher up you go, you stop 'touching' and actively roll up your sleeves to do the implementation, etc. You, instead, focus on strategy and vision for the overall viability and growth of the IT Department.

[116]

Talk It Up! - A Guide To Successful Public Speaking

4. Be A Profit Center
What can you do to bring greater attention to your focus? What can you do to affect the overall effectiveness and profitability of the organization?

Examples
- Build a digital product to show that you are bringing profit to the company. Can you make it easier for clients to view and pay their bills, receive updates and clarify communication channels such as ease of login and security?
- Own a data center and sub out to various divisions or departments and to customers. Leases like rental cars or Airbnb.

5. Become A Resource
Can you provide educational opportunities for the company? Can you implement an online platform, create a how-to guide, or provide training videos on how to use tech more efficiently?

A great talking point: Productivity was at $x\%$ but once we instituted tech training, efficiency and revenue increased by $x\%$ (Intranet training systems).

How can they have a better pulse on technology? They need you as they have to become more digitally savvy.

6. Prepare, Prepare, Prepare
The setting of the conversation: Their office, boardroom but not the hallway or elevator. If you are a C-Suite member, then ask how they would speak with you. Have the same expectation. Keep the conversation in the appropriate context.

Rehearse and take the time to gather information and stick to the facts.

It's helpful to agree on expectations upfront and then summarize, before moving forward with any presentation.

They may tend to be incredibly impatient as their schedules are typically jam-packed — and they have to make lots of high-stakes decisions, often with little time to weigh options. For example, if you are allotted twenty minutes, then prepare as if you only have five minutes. That may end up being the case, so be prepared to crush it regardless of the time you are actually given.

Before presenting, run your talk and your slides by a colleague who will provide honest and pointed feedback. Try to find someone who's had success getting ideas adopted at the executive level. Is your message coming through clearly and quickly?

[117]

Talk It Up! - A Guide To Successful Public Speaking

7. Invest In Yourself

Invest in your own growth in communication. Coaching to help with any speaking anxiety, formation of presentations, and mastering body language. Invest in and stay active with C-Suite and executive mastermind groups. We also have coaching and mastermind groups that would add value to your professional growth.

WORKSHOP 5
Virtual Ice Breakers

More and more of our work is being conducted virtually. This means that you will need to adapt and become more comfortable with this platform. Please note that there is a major difference between speaking personally in front of an audience and speaking virtually to an audience. Just as much energy if not more is needed with this platform. Warming up is essential, especially for speaking virtually as your face becomes the focal point of the meeting. You must be able to clearly pronounce and articulate your message.

If you are the one who is tasked with hosting or facilitating meetings, you may be presented with discovering creative ways to increase engagement. What are some strategies or ways to increase participation? What are some creative 'icebreakers' you can use to help kick off your virtual meeting? Before we look at some of our favorite ice breakers, let us first look at a few helpful tips.

Here are some tips to keep in mind when it comes to incorporating ice breakers and why they can be of incredible value.

- *The more* you get the group to talk, the more engaged they will be. When they are engaged, they are more attentive and tend to retain more because of their experience.
- *Try* these in smaller groups. Can start with or even use these with virtual breakout rooms.
- *Try* a friendly competition and even award a prize or some type of gift. Give them a reason to participate!

Here are some virtual icebreakers you can use for your next virtual presentation or meeting:

1. Name It
Breakout into smaller rooms and come up with a team name. The team with the most creative name as voted on by the attendees, will present last. The team with the least number of votes will present first. If in any way, there is a tie, consider something unique to declare a winner. Perhaps, the team's name that includes or incorporates the breakout room number into their team name wins. For example, a team included their breakout room number in their name, 'One in a Million'.
Time: 3 minutes to work on this (pending the size of the groups)

Talk It Up! - A Guide To Successful Public Speaking

2. Brand The Background

Produce a team custom virtual background (this is a team forming activity). Zoom will allow you to upload an image. Provide Rules: sharing your screen and can use Canva, PowerPoint, Zoom whiteboard, etc. Each team member must have the image uploaded within the time given.

Time: 7 minutes

3. Virtual Networking

Break into pairs of two. Come back and tell them that you are now creating discussion groups/teams. You will now be paired with another group. This time you will need to introduce your partner from the first session with what you learned about them from the previous session.

Time: 5-7 minutes

4. Game Show

This can be a great opening or closing activity. Google Slides/PowerPoint. Use the chat section as the buzzer by teams. Have them type the word 'Buzz' in the chat section and then answer verbally. Can use Jeopardy-type templates. Ask them to please wait until you've read the entire answer before they type into the chat section what their 'question' is. Must give in the form of a question. An incorrect answer means you cannot answer again. Keep your own score. Incorrect answers can lead to a reduction/loss of points or equate to no points at all.

Time: 10-15 minutes

5. Nicknames

Produce virtual nicknames: Tell each other a story from their childhood. The partner comes up with a nickname based on the story for their partner. Now add it to their virtual nickname for all to see. Pick the most creative and ask them to share. You can even tie this into your training.

Time: 4 minutes

6. You've Been Assigned

Give each group an assignment. Recall a life lesson/lesson learned. Provide an example (missed a deadline, lost a deal, etc.). Example assignment: develop a life motto or a department core value statement.

Time: 7 minutes

Reflection

1. *What* are some other icebreaker activities you can use?

WORKSHOP 6
Your Speaker SWOT Analysis

A SWOT analysis is one of many tools an organization may use when developing its marketing and overall business strategies. SWOT is an acronym, and it stands for *Strengths, Weaknesses, Opportunities, and Threats*. You can also use this framework on a personal level to support your own professional development and career goals.

As a part of your Public Speaking Mastery team, we've developed the DSB Leadership Speaking SWOT analysis to support you in making the most of your talents and opportunities. We want to shape and strengthen your brand by understanding what you are excellent at, improve what you would consider to be areas of needed improvement, capitalize on what you can do, and defend against what could be challenging you from becoming the best version of yourself. The first two are primarily internally driven while the latter two are more external. With that in mind, here is how to perform the DSB Leadership SWOT Analysis.

1. Strengths
Start with your goals in mind. Now, think about your personal strengths, skills, and experience and how they will help you achieve your goals. What may be difficult for others is simply second nature to you. These are your competitive advantages. Consider for a moment what others say you do better than anyone else. The ability to communicate effectively and with confidence with colleagues, superiors, employees, and leaders is essential for professional growth.

Consider the following and list as many as you can:

Active listening	Make great eye contact
Empathy	Confidence
Multilingual (speak multiple languages)	Respect
Body language awareness/Positive body language	Vocal tone awareness
Written communication mastery	Storytelling
Persuasive	Diplomacy
Presentation	Negotiation
Authentic	Telephone etiquette
Organizational	Good sense of humor
Passionate	Enthusiasm
Area of expertise	Other

Talk It Up! - A Guide To Successful Public Speaking

2. Weaknesses

Next, think about and list your weaknesses. What could prevent you from achieving your goals? What tasks do you avoid because you don't feel confident doing them? What do other people see as your weaknesses? You might be surprised to learn what they see. You may receive confirmation of what you already know.

Consider the strengths list and the following list:

Lack of confidence	Lack of concentration
Insufficient training	Procrastination
Impatience	Poor relational skills
Speaks quickly	Speaks at a fast pace
Lack of organization	Lack of eye contact
Shaky voice	Presentation delivery
Lack of subject matter understanding	Lack of focus - easily distracted
Unfamiliar with technology	Speaking anxiety

Stutter, or speech impediment (not necessarily a weakness)
Other

3. Opportunities

Now it's time to identify and write down opportunities. Is there a way you could create an opportunity for yourself by taking advantage of one of your strengths, or by eliminating one of your weaknesses? Look at your organization, community, and social circles. Is something happening in the future that could be an opportunity for you?

Recognize and seize opportunities every chance you get. In other words, don't just list opportunities, list who, what, how, and when. Consider applying S.M.A.R.T. goals, which stand for Specific, Measurable, Attainable, Realistic, Timely. Accomplish them and then build from them.

Consider the following and list as many as you can:

Weddings	Small group meetings
Sales pitches (internally & externally)	Church or Faith-Based meetings
Community events	Board meetings
Sales meetings	Team meetings
Staff meetings	Family gatherings
Workshops	Conferences
Event Planners/Network	Other

[122]

Talk It Up! - A Guide To Successful Public Speaking

4. Threats
Next, you need to list the threats that might be standing in the way of your dreams and goals. What obstacles are you facing at work or in your community? Ask again if these are really obstacles or perceived hurdles. What problems could your weaknesses cause, if you don't address them? Are any of your colleagues competing with you for projects or a promotion?

Consider the following and list as many as you can:

Position within your organization	Competition
Technology (new, failure/malfunction)	Time constraints
Lack of distinction/lack of brand depth	Last moment changes
Logistics including room temperature	Event Planners
Audience	Q&A
Preceding or following another presenter	Other

5. Final Step
Finally, look at each of the four lists you created and decide what actions you're going to take to minimize threats, and best take advantage of the opportunities open to you. Highlight anywhere from one to three from each category. These will be more than enough to start with and the most important in achieving (or preventing you from achieving) your public speaking goals. Those identified areas will be your priorities for action.

You are most likely to succeed in life if you use your talents to their fullest extent. Similarly, you'll suffer fewer problems if you know what your weaknesses are and if you manage these weaknesses, they won't matter in the work you do.

So how do you go about identifying these strengths and weaknesses, and analyzing the opportunities and threats that flow from them?

[123]

Talk It Up! - A Guide To Successful Public Speaking

Strengths	Weaknesses	Opportunities	Threats
What are your gifts? What would others consider you to be good at?	What areas do you want to strengthen or improve? What do you want to become more efficient at?	What are some occasions where you can speak? Consider Board meetings, community events, group meetings, weddings, and conferences.	What could hinder your growth? Think both internally and externally.
List Your Strengths	**List Your Weaknesses**	**List All Opportunities**	**List All Threats**

Upon Completion Of The Public Speaking SWOT Analysis
You will be able to identify your speaking personality while defining your speaking mission and value proposition. This will serve not only as a template but also as a confirmation of your competitive advantage. Your talents, strengths, and willingness to go after your weaknesses and opportunities are what will set you apart and bring you to your greatest worth.

So, set aside the proper amount of time to write out your SWOT and then save the document. We ask that you complete this again in the following intervals: 3 months, 6 months and 1 year. This will provide incredible insight into your growth. Remember that the SWOT analysis you conduct will serve to spot opportunities that you didn't know existed or may not have taken advantage of. Additionally, it will identify problems or circumstances that might have a negative effect on your career.

WORKSHOP 7
Your Affirmation List

We've all heard the phrase "you are what you think", and so it goes without saying that the thoughts you entertain about yourself are powerful. Create an Affirmation List and never hold back from telling yourself the truth. Make a list of what you will tell yourself daily. These are positive statements that when repeated often can support positive changes and overcome self-sabotaging and negative thoughts.

Here are a few things to keep in mind when creating your Affirmation List: Use inspiring words and rich vocabulary. These should be words that evoke and trigger the right emotional responses. Keep them in the present tense and try starting with "I am." Post these everywhere to serve as a reminder. Affirmations help to rewire our brains as they produce serotonin, which creates a sense of well-being.

Examples
- I am grateful to be unique. There is no one like me.
- I know, accept and am true to myself.
- I am gifted and talented and choose to use them.
- I believe in, trust and have confidence in myself.
- I choose to see mistakes as learning opportunities.
- I accomplish anything I set my mind to.
- I forgive myself for not being perfect.
- I never give up because it is not in my DNA.
- I accept what I cannot change.
- I make the best of every decision and situation.
- I am courageous.
- I know the power of my brand.
- I am taking good care of my health (mental, physical).
- I am attracting to me positive people.
- I am following my dreams & am doing everything to make them come true.
- I am creating the lifestyle I want.
- I am the best consultant in this niche.
- I am the most qualified to speak about this.
- There are no other fathers who can love (and embarrass) their children like I can.
- I am grateful for my relationships (and express that to them).
- I enjoy providing meaningful and qualified referrals to my partners.

Talk It Up! - A Guide To Successful Public Speaking

- I am better for allowing David to coach me.

Activity
- *Write* your own affirmations and say them out loud throughout the day. Say them until you begin to embrace these truths about yourself.

Acknowledgments

We are grateful for the encouragement we have received from so many people: family, friends, mentors, executives, and members of the speaking and training community. We are blessed to have had so many along our journey impart words of wisdom, lend a helping hand, or extend some of their precious time to listen to two dreamers.

We want to express our appreciation to our clients and to the organizations that have invited us to partner and support their journey, vision, and growth. You are an inspiration to those who desire a greater stage. Thank you for allowing us to share some of your growth journeys - your challenges and victories. You serve as an inspiration for so many who want to be led by courage and not fear and who want to increase their influence.

Steve Cannon for the belief in two young idealistic college students at Howard University all those years ago. Your guidance and support have helped us to mature into the leaders that we are today. We are honored that you wrote the forward for this public speaking guidebook. We cannot thank you enough for your mentorship and belief in us. You modeled inspirational speaking.

Tony Chatman for encouraging me (David) to grow my professional speaking voice.

The members of the various professional communities we are privileged to be a part of. Thank you for providing incredible feedback and for allowing us to share our experiences and material with you.

To Rich Munguia and the team at Elite Public Image for their work and belief in our vision to take our message and make our training readily available for so many.

About The Authors

Danny Suk Brown and David Suk Brown are identical twins and together they co-host the Twins Talk it Up Podcast. Twins Talk it Up is a program focused on entrepreneurship, communication, leadership, and business. They have a combined fifty years of experience with public speaking, having delivered speeches and presentations to groups, workshops, and conferences.

Danny Suk Brown
Danny Suk Brown began his love for public speaking when he was a student at Howard University. Danny served as Mr. School of Engineering and President of the American Society of Mechanical Engineering. He noticed that many professors and students were not comfortable speaking in public and were not able to take very technical terms and simplify them for the audience. He was constantly asked to help prepare both students and professors with their public speaking and presentations.

Today, Danny continues to train and work with business leaders and executives, speaking and training their teams. In addition to providing support to their teams, he also helps these leaders prepare for upcoming keynote speeches and presentations. Danny has also served as the MC at Cloud conferences, Microsoft roadshows, and Fractional Head of Sales for startups.

Danny is an Army Veteran and is the President and owner of AppMeetup, an MSP Training Organization, and a Cloud SaaS Distributor. Danny is also a Co-Founder of Black Channel Partner Alliance (BCPA), an initiative supported by Microsoft to train and build up high-performance, community-focused, channel partners within the technology space.

Danny is married to his wife Jennifer, they have two daughters and reside in Austin, Texas.

David Suk Brown
Known as the Evangelist of Authenticity (#authenticityevangelist), David is not only the President of DSB Leadership Group; he is also an ordained Minister & Evangelist with the Christian Church. With over 25 years of ministry experience, David has had the privilege of leading seven different congregations. He was also instrumental in establishing three additional Church plantings. He continues to support ministries throughout the East and West Coasts.

David is a leadership communications trainer, facilitator, executive coach, and keynote speaker. His background has been in helping organizations with both transitional leadership and leadership development. His niche is in public speaking training and coaching. He is passionate about the development of every organization's greatest resource: its people. He has taught and trained on every platform from mentoring to workshops and Executive Coaching.

David has been married to his wife Leslie for 23 years. They have two children and reside near the US Capital in the metropolitan area of Baltimore, Maryland.

Ways To Find Danny & David

Twins Talk it Up Podcast with Danny Suk Brown & David Suk Brown. Subscribe and download on your favorite platform.

Danny's company 'AppMeetup': https://appmeetup.com/

DSB Leadership Group: http://www.dsbleadershipgroup.com/

Complimentary 15-minute Discovery Conversation: http://www.dsbleadershipgroup.com/schedule-a-call/

25% Discount on a Course when you include within the message or the subject 'Talk it Up': http://www.dsbleadershipgroup.com/contact/

Public Speaking Facebook Group: facebook.com/groups/publicspeakingpoints

Coaching: dsbleadershipgroup.com/executive-coaching-dsb-leadership-group/

Become a Patreon supporter: patreon.com/twinstalkitup

Instagram: @dsbleadershipgroup
Instagram: @twinstalkitup
Twitter: @dsbleadership

LinkedIn: linkedin.com/company/dsbleadershipgroup

Facebook: facebook.com/dsbleadership
Facebook: facebook.com/twinstalkitup

YouTube: https://www.youtube.com/channel/UCL18KYXdzVdzEwMH8uwLf6g/videos

Speech AI Tool: https://www.myvoicevibes.com/

Endnotes

Forward
1. Elder, Cato The. "Quote by Cato The Elder: "Grasp the subject; the words will follow."" *Goodreads*, https://www.goodreads.com/quotes/7679487-grasp-the-subject-the-words-will-follow. Accessed 11 April 2022.
2. "Plato - Rhetoric is the art of ruling the minds of men." *Brainy Quote*, https://www.brainyquote.com/quotes/plato_159589. Accessed 11 April 2022.
3. Carnegie, Dale. "Quote by Dale Carnegie: "There are always three speeches, for every one ..."" *Goodreads*, https://www.goodreads.com/quotes/600722-there-are-always-three-speeches-for-every-one-you-actually. Accessed 11 April 2022.
4. Cannon, Steven and Tresanay. "Guru Wisdom by Steve and Tresanay Cannon." *Goodreads*, https://www.goodreads.com/book/show/30094153-guru-wisdom. Accessed 11 April 2022.

Introduction
1. Schwantes, Marcel, and Robb Holman. "Warren Buffett Says You Will Be Worth 50 Percent More if You Improve This 1 Human Skill." *Inc. Magazine*, 30 March 2020, https://www.inc.com/marcel-schwantes/warren-buffett-says-you-will-be-worth-50-percent-more-if-you-improve-this-1-human-skill.html. Accessed 11 April 2022.
2. Syed, Ali. "Glossophobia: What Is It, Causes, Diagnosis, Treatment, and More." *Osmosis*, https://www.osmosis.org/answers/glossophobia. Accessed 19 April 2022.
3. DSB Leadership Group - Follow us as we lead you into the future, https://www.dsbleadershipgroup.com/. Accessed 11 April 2022.

Chapter 1
1. Emerson, Ralph Waldo. "Quote by Ralph Waldo Emerson: "Speech is power; speech is to persuade..."" *Goodreads*, 23 April 2018, https://www.goodreads.com/quotes/8845136-speech-is-power-speech-is-to-persuade-to-convert-to. Accessed 11 April 2022.
2. Rapp, Christof. "Aristotle's Rhetoric (Stanford Encyclopedia of Philosophy)." *Stanford Encyclopedia of Philosophy*, 2 May 2002, https://plato.stanford.edu/entries/aristotle-rhetoric/. Accessed 11 April 2022.
3. Emerson, Ralph Waldo. "Quote by Ralph Waldo Emerson: "All great speakers were bad speakers at first."" *Goodreads*,

[133]

https://www.goodreads.com/quotes/928083-all-great-speakers-were-bad-speakers-at-first. Accessed 11 April 2022.

Chapter 2
1. Schafer, Sara. "Warren Buffett's 4 Best Tips for Business Leaders." *AgWeb* -, 4 May 2021, https://www.agweb.com/news/business/taxes-and-finance/warren-buffetts-4-best-tips-business-leaders. Accessed 18 April 2022.
2. "Ben Stein - Clear Eyes commercial." *YouTube*, 1 August 2006, https://www.youtube.com/watch?v=RcH-3d-BZn4. Accessed 11 April 2022.
3. "What is Your Vocal Variety Saying About You?" Vocal Impact, 9 December 2011, https://www.vocalimpact.net/2011/12/09/what-is-your-vocal-variety-saying-about-you/. Accessed 11 April 2022.
4. "Twins Talk it Up Episode 24: Facial Communication." *YouTube*, 11 December 2020, https://www.youtube.com/watch?v=LQ8DKAPJJY4. Accessed 19 April 2022.
5. *Sensory Logic: Speaking And Training | Dan Hill*, https://www.sensorylogic.com/. Accessed 23 April 2022.
6. Taylor, Maureen, and Azam Ansari. "3 Ways to Maintain Eye Contact." wikiHow, https://www.wikihow.com/Maintain-Eye-Contact. Accessed 11 April 2022.
7. "Spock | Star Trek." *StarTrek.com*, https://www.startrek.com/database_article/spock. Accessed 19 April 2022.
8. "Strike Zone | Glossary." *MLB.com*, https://www.mlb.com/glossary/rules/strike-zone. Accessed 11 April 2022.
9. "Mehrabian's Communication Theory: Verbal, Non-Verbal, Body Language." *BusinessBalls.com*, 9 June 2017, https://www.businessballs.com/communication-skills/mehrabians-communication-theory-verbal-non-verbal-body-language/. Accessed 11 April 2022.

Chapter 3
1. "Baseball's best batting stances by position." *MLB.com*, 9 December 2021, https://www.mlb.com/news/mlb-all-batting-stance-team. Accessed 18 April 2022.
2. "Wayne Gretzky Quotes - BrainyQuote." Brainy Quote, https://www.brainyquote.com/authors/wayne-gretzky-quotes. Accessed 11 April 2022.

Chapter 4
1. "Admiral McRaven addresses the University of Texas at Austin Class of 2014." *YouTube*, 23 May 2014,

https://www.youtube.com/watch?v=yaQZFhrW0fU. Accessed 11 April 2022.

2. McRaven, William H. "Make Your Bed: Little Things That Can Change Your Life...And Maybe the World by William H. McRaven." *Goodreads*, https://www.goodreads.com/book/show/31423133-make-your-bed. Accessed 11 April 2022.

3. McRaven, William H. "Make Your Bed: Little Things That Can Change Your Life...And Maybe the World by William H. McRaven." *Goodreads*, https://www.goodreads.com/book/show/31423133-make-your-bed. Accessed 11 April 2022.

4. Brown, David Suk. "DSB Affirmation List." *DSB Affirmation List*, https://davidbrown1.podia.com/dsb-affirmation-list. Accessed 11 April 2022.

5. "Undergraduate Courses | Psychological & Brain Sciences." *Johns Hopkins University*, https://pbs.jhu.edu/undergraduate/courses/. Accessed 19 April 2022.

Chapter 5

1. Silva, Laura. "America's Top Fears 2016 - Chapman University Survey of American Fears." *Chapman Blogs*, 11 October 2016, https://blogs.chapman.edu/wilkinson/2016/10/11/americas-top-fears-2016/. Accessed 19 April 2022.

2. "Be Like Mike Gatorade Commercial (ORIGINAL)." *YouTube*, 24 October 2006, https://www.youtube.com/watch?v=b0AGiq9j_Ak. Accessed 12 April 2022.

Chapter 6

1. Covey, Stephen R. "Quote by Stephen R. Covey: "Start with the end in mind. ."" *Goodreads*, https://www.goodreads.com/quotes/25722-start-with-the-end-in-mind. Accessed 18 April 2022.

2. "What if Practice is the Performance: Falling In Love with Practice | Gerald Leonard | TEDxWilmington." *YouTube*, 18 October 2018, https://www.youtube.com/watch?v=xrl2kR2UdHM. Accessed 18 April 2022.

3. Gibbons, Serenity. "You And Your Business Have 7 Seconds To Make A First Impression: Here's How To Succeed." *You And Your Business Have 7 Seconds To Make A First Impression: Here's How To Succeed*, 19 June 2019, https://www.forbes.com/sites/serenitygibbons/2018/06/19/you-have-7-seconds-to-make-a-first-impression-heres-how-to-succeed/?sh=1c72c8b856c2. Accessed 19 April 2022.

Chapter 8

1. "Ben Stein - Clear Eyes commercial." *YouTube*, 1 August 2006, https://www.youtube.com/watch?v=RcH-3d-BZn4. Accessed 11 April 2022.

Chapter 9

1. ""The most powerful person in the world is the story teller. The storyteller sets the vision, values and agenda of an entire generation that is to come." Steve Jobs." *JovanaBanovic*, 6 August 2020, http://jovanabanovic.com/2020/08/06/the-most-powerful-person-in-the-world-is-the-story-teller-the-storyteller-sets-the-vision-values-and-agenda-of-an-entire-generation-that-is-to-come-steve-jobs/. Accessed 11 April 2022.

2. Peterson, Bob. "Disney Pixar UP." *Disney Movies*, 29 May 2009, https://movies.disney.com/up. Accessed 18 April 2022.

3. "The magical science of storytelling | David JP Phillips | TEDxStockholm." *YouTube*, 16 March 2017, https://www.youtube.com/watch?v=Nj-hdQMa3uA. Accessed 11 April 2022.

Chapter 10

1. *VoiceVibes - VoiceVibes*, https://www.myvoicevibes.com/. Accessed 19 April 2022.

2. "Twins Talk it Up Episode 31: Improve your voice with AI." *YouTube*, 23 January 2021, https://www.youtube.com/watch?v=tHyy-uyrkY0. Accessed 19 April 2022.

Chapter 11

1. Taylor, Amanda. "It's More Than Just Talk: Patterns of CEO Impromptu Communication." *Academia.edu*, https://www.academia.edu/11775175/It_s_More_Than_Just_Talk_Patterns_of_CEO_Impromptu_Communication. Accessed 11 April 2022.

2. "MLB World Series: Historical winners and highlights." *MLB.com*, https://www.mlb.com/postseason/history/world-series. Accessed 19 April 2022.

3. "Grand Slam (GSH) | Glossary." *MLB.com*, https://www.mlb.com/glossary/standard-stats/grand-slam. Accessed 19 April 2022.

Chapter 12

1. Lydgate, John. "Quote by John Lydgate: "You can please some of the people all..."" *Goodreads*, https://www.goodreads.com/quotes/699462-you-can-please-some-of-the-people-all-of-the. Accessed 11 April 2022.

Workshop 1 | Imposter Syndrome

1. Sakulku, J. "The Impostor Phenomenon". *The Journal of Behavioral Science*, vol. 6, no. 1, Oct. 2011, pp. 75-97, doi:10.14456/ijbs.2011.6.

2. Angelou, Maya. "Quote by Maya Angelou: "Each time I write a book, every time I face tha..."" *Goodreads*, https://www.goodreads.com/quotes/220406-each-time-i-write-a-book-every-time-i-face. Accessed 12 April 2022.

3. Gorman, Gus, and Richard Pryor. "Kryptonite | Superman Wiki | Fandom." *Superman Wiki*, https://superman.fandom.com/wiki/Kryptonite. Accessed 19 April 2022.
4. "Five Second Rule | Highbrow." *GoHighBrow*, 5 April 2017, https://gohighbrow.com/five-second-rule/. Accessed 20 April 2022.
5. *Nike. Just Do It. Nike.com*, https://www.nike.com/. Accessed 19 April 2022.
6. Ross, Herbert, director. *The Secret of My Success*. Performance by Michael J. Fox, 1987. Accessed 19 April 2022.
7. "Start With Why." *Simon Sinek*, https://simonsinek.com/product/start-with-why/?ref=home. Accessed 19 April 2022.
8. "Why You Get Imposter Syndrome And How to Overcome It...with Dr. Tara Swart" *eJOY English*, https://ejoy-english.com/go/video/why-you-get-imposter-syndrome-and-how-to-overcome-it-inc/62569. Accessed 20 April 2022.
9. Clance, PhD. Pauline R. "Imposter Phenomenon." *Dr. Pauline Rose Clance - Imposter Phenomenon*, 2013, https://paulineroseclance.com/impostor_phenomenon.html. Accessed 19 April 2022.
10. Brown, David, and Danny Brown. "Twins Talk it Up Episode 16: Conquering Imposter Syndrome." *YouTube*, 22 September 2020, https://www.youtube.com/watch?v=swJg2eX_ZCI. Accessed 22 April 2022.

Workshop 2 | What pros do and don't do
1. McClure, Bruce. "What is an astronomical unit? | Space." *EarthSky*, 23 October 2017, https://earthsky.org/space/what-is-the-astronomical-unit/. Accessed 19 April 2022.

Workshop 4 | Speaking with the C-Suite
1. "What is the DiSC assessment? - DiSC Profile." Discprofile.com, https://www.discprofile.com/what-is-disc. Accessed 11 April 2022.

Additional Resources

Chapter 1
Aristotle's Rhetoric - https://plato.stanford.edu/entries/aristotle-rhetoric/

Chapter 2
Eye contact anxiety - https://www.wikihow.com/Maintain-Eye-Contact

Chapter 4
Your Affirmation List - https://davidbrown1.podia.com/dsb-affirmation-list

Chapter 6
TEDx - Gerald Leonard - 'What if Practice is the Performance?'
https://www.ted.com/talks/gerald_j_leonard_what_if_practice_is_the_performance_falling_in_love_with_practice or find it on YouTube here: https://www.youtube.com/watch?v=xrl2kR2UdHM

Chapter 9
'The Magical Science of Storytelling' - David JP Phillips
https://www.youtube.com/watch?v=Nj-hdQMa3uA

Workshop | Imposter Syndrome
'Clance IP Scale' - Pauline Clance
https://paulineroseclance.com/impostor_phenomenon.html
https://paulineroseclance.com/pdf/IPTestandscoring.pdf

Workshop | Speaking with the C-Suite
DiSC assessment - https://www.discprofile.com/what-is-disc

Index

Affirmations... 45, 125-6
Always (Never) Statements... 65
Amanda Taylor... 81
Anett D. Grant... 81
Anxiety, (See Nerves)... 6, 13-14, 25, 39-44, 52, 59, 88, 109, 117, 122, 139
Aristotle... 2, 29, 133, 139
Aristotle's *Rhetoric*... 2, 29, 133, 139
Awards... 94

Barack Obama, President... iv, 92
Batting Stance... 28, 61, 77, 88, 95-6, 99, 107
Ben Stein... 10, 67
Body Language... 11-20, 28, 41, 58, 60, 69-72, 95, 107, 112, 117, 121, 134
    Eye Contact... 13-15, 22-3, 25, 91, 108, 134, 139
    Hands... 15-18, 24, 37, 39, 40, 85, 87, 107
    Arms...15-17, 25, 44
Breathing (Techniques)... 43-44, 65, 85
Brene Brown... 103
Business and Professional Communication Quarterly... 81

C-Suite... 84, 115-118
Cadence... 66-7, 112
Chapman University... 39, 135
Charts/Graphs... 18, 79
Clance IP Scale... 104, 137, 139
Clear Eyes (Drops) ... 10, 67, 134-5
Closes... 50, 54, 112

Dan Hill... 12
David JP Phillips... 70, 136, 139

Debra Cancro... 76
DISC Assessment... 115, 137
DSB Leadership Group... 53, 60, 65, 76, 79, 81, 96, 99, 112, 129, 131
Elevator Pitch... 111-113
Elite Public Image... 127
Empathy... 95
Energy... 25, 27-8, 37, 40-1, 45, 54, 58, 67, 109, 119
Eric Thomas... iv, 107
Eulogies... iii

Fear... iii, 13, 33, 39-42, 101-2, 127, 135
Feedback... 43, 53-5, 57-60, 80-1, 89-90, 103, 117, 127
Filler Words... 63-6, 76
Forbes... 53, 135

Gatorade... 45, 135
Gerald Leonard... 53, 135, 139
Google (Slides)... 77, 120
Gratitude... 35, 94, 102-3

Harvard Review... 52
Humor... 54, 85, 96

Ice Breakers (Virtual)... 119-120
International Journal of Behavioral Science... 101, 136
Imposter Syndrome... 52, 101-5, 136-7, 139
Impromptu Talks (Speeches)... 81-88
Interviews... 14, 48, 69, 81

Jack Canfield... 107
Johns Hopkins University... 35, 135
John Lydgate... 93, 136

Les Brown... iv, 27

Maya Angelou... 101, 136
Meetings... 14, 21, 41, 47, 61, 81, 84, 116, 119
Mehrabian's 7-38-55 Rule... 19, 134
Mentimeter... 76
Metronome (App) ... 76
Michael J. Fox... 103, 136
Michael Jordan... 104
Microphone... 36, 74, 85-86, 91
Microsoft Teams... 76, 129
Mindset... 22, 26, 28, 33, 42-46, 60, 65

Nerves (See Anxiety)... 6, 13-14, 25, 39-44, 52, 57, 59, 88, 109, 117, 122, 139
Networking... 11, 120
Never (Always) Statements... 65
Nike... 103, 136
Nonverbal Language... 9, 11-18

Objectives (Handling)... 34, 116
Openings... 50-1, 53, 55, 60, 120

Pacing... 12, 109
    On Stage... 12, 42
    Speaking/Presenting... 12, 59, 109
Pauline Clance... 104, 137, 139
Pause (Power of)... 29-30, 45, 64-67, 82, 86, 90
Pitch (Variations)... 10, 111-113
Presence... 15, 17, 79, 96
Podcast... 12, 48, 76, 96, 105, 129, 131
PowerPoint (PowerPoint 3D)... 36, 76-7, 108, 120
PromptSmart Lite (Teleprompter)... 76

Q&A (Sessions)... 55, 86, 96

Ralph Waldo Emerson... 1, 7, 133

Rehearsing... 57, 60
Relaxation Techniques... 16-17, 36, 38, 44-5, 58, 109
Rich Munguia... 127

Sensory Logic ... 12, 134
Simon Sinek... 103, 137
Slides... 18-19, 24, 36, 57, 61, 74, 76-9, 108, 117, 120
Speaking Anxiety... 6, 14, 25, 36, 39, 109, 117, 122
Start with Why... 103, 136
Stephen Covey... 47, 135
Steven Cannon... i-ii
Steve Jobs... 69, 134
Skype... 76, 137
Star Trek... 15, 134
Star Wars... 15
Structure (Speech) ... 49-55

Tara Swart... 104, 137
TEDx... 53, 135-6, 139
Teleprompter... 76
Timing... 55, 76
Toast (Delivery)... 84-5
Toastmaster (Timer)... 76
Tone... 10-11, 19, 67, 107, 112, 121
Tony Chatman... 127
Tony Robbins ... iv, 27, 107

Ummo... 65, 76

Verbal Language... 9-11, 19, 34
Virtual Platforms... 76
Visual Aids... 18, 36, 43, 48, 57, 79
Visualization... 33-8, 45, 53-4, 58-9, 102
VoiceVibes... 76, 131, 136
Vocal Variety... 10, 58, 60, 63, 66, 67, 134

Wayne Gretzky... 31, 134
William H. McRaven, Gen.... 33, 134

Zoom... 76, 120

Made in the USA
Columbia, SC
14 February 2024

31544814R00088